# The UPSIDE of DOWN

# The UPSIDE of DOWN

## A New Perspective on Reality, Choices and the Pursuit of Happiness

FIRST EDITION

KRISTINE DEXHEIMER

PARSLEY PUBLISHING

First Edition

Cover Art Created by Gary Dexheimer.
Copyright © 2011 by Kristine Dexheimer

Library of Congress Cataloging-In-Publication Data
Dexheimer, Kristine.
The Upside of Down: A New Perspective on Reality, Choices and the Pursuit of Happiness /Kristine Dexheimer -- 1st ed.
     p.  cm.          LCCN 2011943198

ISBN 978-0-9838649-0-5

www.parsleypublishing.com

For Kenny and Sheila

THE BEEHIVE

Books take a team to create. This book is no exception. Although it seems entirely inadequate, I would like to thank:

The Snowman
My mom, my safety net
Michelle for publicity and promotion
Haley for typesetting and interpretation
Gary for chemo companionship and cover art
Julie for conviction, editing and encouragement
Rae for commas, quotation marks and capitalization
Swantje for organizing the pieces into a beautiful quilt
Ethan for artwork, confidence, faith and trying hot lunch
To the many others who helped make this book a reality, "thank you."

To everyone who reserved a copy before it existed,
I dedicate this edition to you.

# CONTENTS

## DEDICATION

This book is dedicated to you – the reader.
And to cancer who drove me ever onward
and left me no retreat.

*Only those things are beautiful which are inspired by madness and written by reason.*

———— Andre Gide

CHAPTER 1

THE BEGINNING

REALITY

According to a probability chart, I'm dying. While aimlessly wandering through life I stumbled and fell face first into my own mortality. I came up dripping with death or at least the fear of it. From this new vantage point I could see the end, but I could also see the beginning. More notably, I had an entirely new perspective on that small space in between the two — that space we call life.

Coming to terms with the realization that I'm dying has left me scarred, battered, tired and forever grateful. In the space of a year, my entire life had been turned upside-down. I journeyed deep within my psyche. I battled monsters and temptations, both real and imagined. I swallowed the bittersweet pill of mortality. Physically, I morphed into a pale, pasty and hairless creature I no longer recognized — Darth Vader without his mask. Mentally, emotionally and spiritually I had no idea who I was anymore.

What did it all mean? As I cursed my misfortune and brooded over my fate, the word *realize* swam clockwise through my mind. It jabbed relentlessly at my consciousness until I reached up high, to the top of a dusty bookcase in my library. I moved the Hilo ukulele we bought at a pawn shop on Maui out of the way. I heaved down my Webster's New International Dictionary with Reference History — the India paper edition circa 1921. I thumbed gingerly through the yellowed pages as thin as onion skin. Here we are — *realize*. According to Webster, *realize* has seven meanings. I was struck not so much by the various meanings of *realize*, but by the omission of the one thing I thought *realize* stood for, namely, to understand.

Listed below are the seven meanings of *realize* according to my ever faithful companion Noah Webster.
1.  To make real; to convert from the imaginary or fictitious into the actual; to bring into concrete existence; to accomplish
2.  To cause to seem real; to impress upon the mind as actual
3.  To verify
4.  To conceive vividly as real; to apprehend clearly
5.  To experience
6.  To convert into actual money
7.  To acquire as an actual possession; to obtain as the result of plans and efforts

As I looked back over all of the various meanings of *realize*, one theme stood out above all others — every definition required *action*. To make, to accomplish, to cause, to verify, to conceive, to experience, to convert or to acquire. For most people I'm probably splitting hairs here, but for me, the significance of this revelation could literally mean the difference between life and death. *Realizing* that the power to mold reality lay in *my* hands was the first *Upside of Down*.

I understood the concept of death and all of the ramifications that went along with it. That's what I thought *realize* meant — to passively accept my fate. However, according to Webster, I had much more control than that. I had the capacity to choose whether to make a probability chart my reality or not.

I began to think differently. Perhaps a hope was just a hope, a fear was just a fear, a plan just a plan and a probability just a probability unless I verified that information as fact, conceived it vividly as real, and impressed that chance upon my mind as truth — in other words, unless I fulfilled it.

My consciousness shifted. No longer would I submissively accept the fulfillment of a computer-generated probability chart as real. My first lesson was to adopt an attitude of deliberate choice in realizing my fate.

## DEATH

I never much thought about death — certainly not my own. Recently I began interrogating myself daily. *What do I know about death? If I did everything the doctors asked of me would I still die? What would death feel like? Would it hurt? Would I be scared? Do I really have a choice in the matter? If I died would my husband remarry? Who would raise my son? Would he call her mom? He's so young, would he even remember me? If I died and some other woman waltzed into my role would I haunt her relentlessly?* Yes!  The certainty of that fact gave me comfort and for the first time in many weeks the corners of my mouth curled upward.

Eventually I surmised that I wasn't actively dying. Even if I were, death came like a slow leak. It would be a while until all the life force had left my body. I was, instead, making dinner and doing laundry. Later I would read our son a story. In the morning I would make love with my husband before looking in the mirror bewildered at the hairless crone I had become. My probability chart, the one I created, stated that chances are I wouldn't be caught up in the throes of dying for quite some time. Slowly, I began to live.

In my life, I had encountered a handful of people near death. They knew it. When I looked into their eyes, I knew it, too. Still we often choose to lie to ourselves and those we love instead of facing the music, but that's another story.

Occasionally I'm still terrified that I might be nearing the end of my life. When this happens the first thing I do is ask myself some pointed questions:

*Am I going to die this instant?* If I'm relatively sure that the answer is no, I take a deep breath and continue. *How about today? Do I really think I'm going to kick-off today?* No. I begin to relax. *If I spend the whole day worrying that I might be dying, can I prevent the grim reaper from coming?* No. Finally I show myself a little tough love. I ask myself; *if I love my life so much why not get on with living it?* So, I do, and in the process, I feel better. *Besides, I can't die*, I remind myself, *I haven't even lived yet.* You could say I spent my days playing it safe, sitting in an overstuffed chair in the foyer of life.

*I can't imagine what it's like to be a convict,*
*but I think in some real way, we're all prisoners.*

———— Shirley Partridge

*Most people live,
whether physically,
intellectually or morally,
in a very restricted
circle of their potential being.
They make use of a very small
portion of their possible
consciousness, and of their
soul's resources in general,
much like a man who,
out of his whole bodily
organism, should get into
the habit of using and
moving only his little finger.
Great emergencies and crises
show us how much greater
our vital resources are
than we had supposed.*

———— William James

CHAPTER 2

# THE FOYER

In high school I read a short story by Frank Stockton called The Lady or the Tiger. The story has a fairy tale quality. Fairy tales have a way of rolling around inside my head until a deeper significance reveals itself in the reflected light of contemplation.

In The Lady or the Tiger a handsome and virtuous man falls in love with the princess of the land. Keep in mind, she's a princess and used to having her way. Her dad, the king, loves his daughter very much; however, he forbids her to marry this poor yet noble man.

The king, being a sporting man, sets up an arena for the amusement of the inhabitants of the kingdom. The arena contains identical soundproof doors. Behind one door awaits a beautiful maiden whom the jealous princess loathes. If our hero chooses that door, he and the maiden will marry and live happily ever after. Behind the second door awaits a ferocious man-eating tiger. If our hero chooses this door, he's tiger meat.

The princess has outwitted her father. (Or has she?) At any rate, she has discovered which door conceals the lady and which door hides the tiger. As her lover enters the arena to face his fate, she almost imperceptibly motions for him to choose the door on the right. Without hesitation he walks to the right and casts open the door. The reader is left to imagine the fate of our hero.

Since my days in high school, my philosophy — the way I lived my life — had been to choose... neither. I liked to sit back and wait. If I refused to choose, both options remained possible. What I failed to consider was that neither option actually existed — not really. Both options held potential, but neither happened. Nothing happened. I lived with my dreams, my possibilities, but did nothing to bring them to fruition. I couldn't fail, but I couldn't succeed either.

Thus as my story began, I sat in a stale, windowless foyer of life and enjoyed a peanut butter and jelly sandwich on white bread. This small space had been my home for years. Although I didn't feel much like reading, I left the reading lamp on. As my sole source of light, it was always on. The only way to leave this self-imposed prison was through a door into the unknown, so I stayed.

In a dimly lit room of faded floral walls, threadbare carpets, and dust, I sat in a drab, overstuffed chair. A small box rested near my feet. Mirrors completely lined one wall. I gazed from a safe distance at the twin portals of Fate and Possibility. I feared the doors would somehow open. Once a gateway opened, I knew it could never again be closed. So I diligently watched.

The box at my feet was left over from college. A relatively small box, it contained a cat. Not just any cat, this cat previously belonged to Schrödinger. When he gave me the box he claimed that the cat inside was both alive and dead. "Open it," he suggested.

Only upon my observation would the cat exist exclusively in one condition or the other. If I didn't open the box I could kid myself into believing that the cat lived a happy and healthy life in there. I hadn't fed or given this cat water in over two decades. If I allowed myself to think about it, I was pretty sure the cat was dead. Still, I refused to open the box because inside the closed box the cat could still be alive. I told myself that only if I looked at him would I kill him for certain. I didn't want his blood on my hands and so, I did nothing.

Loneliness and Fear kept me company. Yearning for something more, my withered soul hummed a woeful ballad. The somber music attracted attention. A tiny creature slipped undetected through the cracks in my foundation and darted across the tattered floor. She came nearer. Then nearer still. She resembled a spider. *Is that a doctor's bag she's carrying?* Somehow, I knew that she had come to kill me or to save me. The choice would be entirely mine.

I lifted my feet off the floor and squeezed my body back hoping to disappear into the upholstery. She scuttled up the leg of my chair. She moved quickly over my body. My neck. My face. She opened her mouth. A long white tongue rolled out and she tasted the air. She gleamed with anticipation. Then, as quickly as she arrived, she was gone. I felt a twinge in my chest. *Ach, it's nothing,* I told myself. Meanwhile, inside my chest, she plunged her thin legs into the fallow fields of my body, and began to grow. For two years, I did nothing.  My husband noticed the lump. We sloughed off our concern by claiming I probably had torn a muscle.  If I didn't admit that something was wrong — if I didn't open that box — then, it wasn't true.

While I sat and waited, she grew larger and more powerful. I didn't welcome her, but I didn't force her to leave either.

When she became strong enough, she spoke. "You know me," she began, "and I know you."

"I know you?" I puzzled. "How?"

"You were born under my sign, as was your father before you."

I had always considered myself a birthday present for my dad although in true form, I arrived a day late. We were both born in the beginning of July. We were both born under the Zodiac sign of Cancer. My head reeled as the blood suddenly retreated from my extremities. I leapt from the chair and studied my reflection in the wall of mirrors.

Something in my face registered her presence.

"I'm a… Cancer," I hesitantly answered. At once I knew she was right. "You killed my father!" I exploded. "And my uncle, and my grandmother!"

For years I thought I was safe in my comfy chair where nothing bad could reach me, but it could. It did. I resolved that it really didn't matter which door I chose. I couldn't just sit in the lobby of life any longer.

I decided first to open the small box near my feet and kill Schrödinger's cat once and for all. Experiencing the real sight and smell of a cat that's been dead and stored in a box for over twenty years has got to be better than no experiences at all.

I had spent life hidden away — hidden behind dreams, fears, food, television, other people's drama and now illness. I silently screamed, *No more!* I chose to experience life — to do something, anything, or to die trying.

As for the doors, like our hero in *The Lady or the Tiger*, I picked the door on the right. I turned the knob. The hinges, corroded from time and neglect, loudly protested. I pushed. The door moaned. I hit it hard with my shoulder and the door gave-way. I dashed across the threshold without looking back. Once on the other side, everything went black.

*The first and best victory is to conquer self.*
*To be conquered by self is, of all things,*
*the most shameful and vile.*

——— Plato

## CHAPTER 3

## ILLUSIONS

Eventually my eyes adjusted to the darkness. I turned around, but the doorway, the floral wallpaper, even the over-stuffed beige chair were gone. I continued on — down a dimly lit hallway. The air hung damp and low.

On my right cages stretched out before me as far as I could see. Each cage held a treadmill. On each treadmill someone walked alone and indifferent. At the front of each treadmill a television created the illusion of movement. The blue-gray glow from the TV screens created long, grim shadows.

No one seemed aware of our dismal surroundings. Perhaps they were sleepwalking. One thing is certain, they were not conscious.

Something familiar caught my eye. I stopped dead in my tracks and pressed back into the cold, cement wall. I had recognized one of the mindless creatures. It was me, or more accurately, my body.

*How had my life been reduced to this?*

The door to the cage was open. I tentatively stepped inside. In an effort to save myself, I quietly guided my body off of the treadmill — half-expecting a loud alarm to sound. Nothing happened. None of the others even looked up. Only my body gazed at me blankly before attempting to free itself and step back onto the treadmill.

For a moment I considered letting it. Perhaps I should just continue going nowhere? After all, I'm lazy and indifferent by nature. However, I didn't want this to be my life… dim, colorless and invisible. I broke into a cold sweat as I yanked my body toward the door of the cage.

Fearing I would lose my nerve, I pulled myself into the hallway as quickly as possible. At the far end of the hall I could see a short flight of stairs and an emergency exit. I slid along the wall in the direction of that door, and dragged my body behind me. I noticed that all the cage doors were open.

"Stop!" I screamed at all of my fellow captives. "You don't have to stay here!"

But, no one could hear me — or perhaps no one wanted to. I didn't know which, but I knew I had to get out. I continued forward.

Once at the top of the stairs, I leaned hard into the lever mechanism. The door opened and my body fell out onto a green field bathed in sunlight. I tripped and fell into myself, my mind and body reuniting.

I lay breathless, yet awake and aware. For the first time in many years, I experienced entirely, the soft warmth of sunlight. I soaked it in as the tender grass caressed my body.

My thoughts turned to the nothingness I had just escaped. A twinge of sorrow pierced my heart. *Why couldn't anyone hear me?* I guess, maybe each person's mind has to rescue his or her own body from the treadmill. It probably wouldn't have been good if I took a whole bunch of bodies up to the light without their minds anyway. I placed my hands behind my head. I lay back and closed my eyes. I committed to my own wellbeing. Although it wouldn't be easy, I decided it was worth the time and energy needed to regain my health. Endless possibilities awaited me in the sun now that I had escaped my own apathy.

I used to think, *oh, I couldn't possibly,* or, *I have no time for that.*

*That's not a real job. I'm not smart enough. I'm not creative enough. I'm not good enough. I'm not... I'm not... I'm not...*

But, just maybe I am. At any rate, I've got nothing to lose. I'd rather die trying, than die never having experienced life. In the blink of an eye anything and everything became possible. Both nothing and everything had changed. I opened a door — the door of possibilities. What was I so afraid of? Why did I wait so long?

৶৩

I alone created my prison of should and should nots, of musts and ought-tos, and so has everybody else. I know now that I am responsible for my life and the choices I make.

Off to my left I heard a voice. "The journey of discovery begins with one step."

I glanced in the direction of the voice. In the distance a turtle sat near a tinkling stream. She winked at me and vanished.

I felt — different, stronger. I decided I could face my illness.

My husband wouldn't be home until Saturday. That gave me three days to prepare for the impending conversation and the whirlwind of activity that would certainly follow.

I made up my mind. Determined to confront my assailant, I made an appointment with the doctor. Although he could help, I knew to rid her from my body completely, I would have to fight the noblest of all battles — the one against myself.

*Better stay away from him*
*He'll rip your lungs out, Jim*
*I'd like to meet his tailor*
*Ahhhhhhooooooooooo*

Werewolves of London ——————— Warren Zevon

CHAPTER 4

# THE WEREWOLF

Doctors, nurses and technicians all took a good look at the lump now growing rapidly inside my chest. They squashed it, X-rayed it, harpooned it and, finally, sent a piece of it off to a lab for further investigation. All concurred that it was approximately the size of a quail's egg. All concurred it was unmistakably cancer.

*Simple enough,* I tried to convince myself. I'll just go have a surgeon take it out and be done with it.

Then on some random Tuesday in June, I met the surgeon face to face. His dark, straight hair leaned back in tidy perfection. His impeccably scrubbed, well-manicured nails glimmered in the harsh, fluorescent light of the examining room. *I wonder if he waxes his knuckles. His fingers are so pink.*

The surgeon had quite a different outlook on the situation. "Your breasts have betrayed you," he informed me rather matter-of-factly.

Gary, my husband, let out an audible gasp.

The surgeon shot a cold, impersonal glance his way. "If you live long enough, your prostate will betray you too," he added.

Without awaiting a response, he shifted his attention back to me. His manner implied that his time was extremely valuable and limited. He hastily ran down the options — take off one breast, take them both, take a lump plus radiation. Chemo? Maybe or maybe not (we'll see); oh, and even if I had them both removed I could still be looking at chemo and/or radiation.

I didn't respond. I couldn't. I wasn't listening. I liked my boobies and wanted to keep them both. I wanted to run away to — anywhere. To nowhere. But the surgeon droned on. He became visibly agitated by my lack of response. His approach grew increasingly provoking. After all, I was wasting his valuable time.

I shut down. Not intentionally. More like a meltdown. Perhaps I blew a breaker. All I know is that I could no longer hear the surgeon. I watched his mouth move as I'm sure he described many wonderful treatments. My ears turned hot and red. In self-preservation, they curled in on themselves to form small seashells. All I could hear was the ocean or the whooshing of my blood as it coursed through my arteries. For the first time, since this whole thing started, I felt sick. I shrank back inside myself. I tried to speak, but no words reached the surface.

From a safe distance inside my protective shell, I stared at the surgeon's hair. *It's so — wolfish,* I thought. I then stared hard at his mouth. I tried to concentrate, but the words didn't seem to match up with the movement of his lips. *Don't trust him. He's really a werewolf,* I advised myself.

As I tried to make sense of it all, I pictured the werewolf and I having a piña colada together at Trader Vic's. Instead of listening to him drone on, I watched inside my mind as he clumsily tried to grasp his glass with pudgy, pink fingers. *Keep him close. Don't let him out of your sight.*

Finally, to my delight, he stopped talking. For a moment the words continued to swirl and spin through the disinfected clinic. Then even the words stopped. The nurse, the werewolf and my husband sat frozen.

All eyes were on me.

Eventually I heard a voice, low and calm, "What if I choose — nothing?" Although the words had passed over my lips, the voice sounded far-off and foreign to me.

"Then we will take your husband into another room and get you some psychiatric help. It is not an option!" The surgeon rubbed his palms briskly on the thighs of his pants. His yellow eyes flared as he exhaled loudly in exasperation.

Although it wasn't my intention, I had succeeded in angering the werewolf. I'm sure he had convinced himself that brutality served these types of situations best. Perhaps he believed the quicker I reached despair, the quicker I could begin to climb back out.

I, however, found the ceaseless bombardment suffocating. I watched in agony as he assaulted the small child who lives inside my heart. She just sat on her lotus flower in the middle of my chest and slowly lost consciousness. He continued to verbally beat her down, all the way down, until nothing remained. No good options. No way out. I decided I didn't want to reach his version of reality. I just wanted to go home.

My mascara burned my eyes. Confused, discouraged, scared and not just a little pissed-off, I didn't really feel much like scaling the walls of self-pity. Cancer wasn't going at all the way I had planned. I refused to hear another word. In frustration, I tried to scream, but couldn't find my voice.

After many moments I found two words I could say to end the assault. I swallowed hard. I choked back my assessment of the man and of the situation.

"Thank you," I muttered.

I couldn't see very well and groped around with trembling hands. The cool, lumpy, plastic of the chair beneath my legs felt good. I grasped the seat firmly to steady my legs. I stood. My breaths came shallow and too quickly to catch. Snot covered my upper lip and chin. Hives dotted my chest. With the teaspoon of grace and dignity I had left, I put on my sunglasses and staggered toward the door.

Once outside I begged Gary to drive really fast. "Make my ears fly back," I requested.

"Where to?" he asked.

"Away," I replied. I rolled down the window and lay my aching head on the door frame. I envisioned us outrunning the doctor's words. As we drove, my breathing slowed. My hives lightened. Eventually even my tears dried up.

Yeah, I already had all the answers. What I hadn't realized is that all the answers I had were wrong. Soon, Cancer would teach me to question — everything.

*If we win here we will win everywhere.*
*The world is a fine place and worth the fighting for*
*and I hate very much to leave it.*

For Whom the Bell Tolls ———— Ernest Hemingway

CHAPTER 5

## CHOICES

I had a choice to make. And, frankly, all the options sucked. I considered once again choosing not to choose, but this time that tactic just might kill me. Every option came at a steep price. I could no longer do nothing. I knew I had to find a path and take it. If I didn't, I would be dragged along by my hair in a direction not of my choosing. Would I go a conventional or an alternative route? I weighed my options carefully. I knew whichever choice I made must be worth the price. I took my time deciding. I listened to all the advice offered. I didn't know which voice to trust. I couldn't tell fear from reason. Then a memory came crashing back. A memory of life and death. A memory of cancer and probabilities.

> *To wake the soul by tender strokes of art,*
> *To raise the genius, and to mend the heart;*
> *To make mankind, in conscious virtue bold,*
> *Live o'er each scene, and be what they behold:*
> *For this the tragic muse first trod the stage.*

——————— Alexander Pope

## History Repeats

The year was 1975. I bounded up the stairs from school. We lived on the second floor above an old grocery store with wooden floors and tin ceilings. Mom called for me. I just knew she wanted to tell me that they had finally decided to buy me a pony. Instead, she was crying. My dad lay calmly in a mushroom-colored, faux fur chaise lounge in our harvest-gold living room. As he relaxed, my mom spoke through her sobs. "We went to see the doctor today," she began. "Daddy has cancer."

I remembered thinking, *No pony?*

Dad didn't look like he was dying — not that I had any idea what a dying man was supposed to looked like. He looked more like a tan, youngish Santa Claus. He drove a milk truck for a living. Most truck drivers had CB radios back then. He was no exception. On the citizen-band airwaves he was known as the Snowman. It fit.

I lay down next to him. We didn't talk. We didn't cry. He just closed his eyes and buried his nose in my hair.

In the morning he woke me early. "Instead of going to school today, let's go fishing," he said.

Soon the doctors ran out of viable treatment options. The prognosis was bleak — six months tops. The Snowman stopped going to the doctor. He instead filled his days with family and fishes.

For years we waited for death to arrive. I missed a lot of school, and we did a lot of fishing. We clung to life and to each other. We made the most of the time we had together. It would take death another twenty years to arrive. It was still too soon.

Several years after the Snowman, his younger brother, Squint, received a hauntingly similar diagnosis. I secretly rejoiced for my cousins. After all, in my mind, it was now their turn to miss lots of school and spend lots of time with their dad.

Like the Snowman, Uncle Squint's diagnosis was terminal. Lots of people cried for him. They cried too for his wife and his kids like they had for us. *None of that meant he would actually die,* I thought. I had heard all of this before.

My Grandpa Bob came down from the Wisconsin North Woods to spend some time with his son. I don't remember him doing that for Dad. I must have appeared indifferent, because he decided that he would celebrate my fifteenth birthday with me instead of going to the hospital that day.

Grandpa Bob was usually a gruff and grumpy man. He owned a hotel and tavern almost four hours north of us. He was a busy man with no time or patience for children. He scared me. His temper flared high and terrible with little provocation. I really wasn't overly thrilled to spend my birthday with my grumpy grandpa, but how could I refuse?

For my birthday, he invited me on a bus tour — just the two of us. The local tavern offered a gambling trip from our hometown to the Arlington Park Racetrack just north of Chicago. While en route, we could enjoy alcoholic beverages and snacks. Grandpa let me order a brandy old-fashioned sweet with pickled mushrooms. I slammed it to calm my nerves.

Once at the track Grandpa allowed me to play the ponies. I could bet up to three dollars per race and he would foot the bill. Most times I lost, but on the fourth race I won eleven dollars. He let me keep my winnings.

Despite my apprehension, we had a wonderful time. For this one day, we were — friends. We didn't speak of dads or sons or cancer, but somehow I knew that Uncle Squint would not be coming home from the hospital. I knew that for my cousins, terminal cancer would not mean missed school and fishing trips; and for my grandpa, it would mean the loss of his son.

Uncle Squint died just over a month later.

Cancer arrived and grew during the same stage of life for the Snowman, for Uncle Squint and now for me. For each of us the cancer began close to the heart — over the heart.

*How could this happen in the same way, in the same family, for three different people and in two consecutive generations?* I wondered.

In the end, I couldn't answer that question. No one could. Asking the question didn't change my prognosis in the least. I resolved instead, to find a way to stop history from repeating itself. I couldn't bear the thought of my son telling my eight-year-old granddaughter about cancer, and a simple probability chart that stated, in black and white, that he too, had a ninety-nine percent chance he would not live to see her grow-up.

"Dear God," I began to pray. I prayed to all gods, but to no god in particular. My relationship with God is... complicated. I believe in a supreme architect of everything, but to whom does he belong? Each religion claims exclusivity on the matter. For now, I needed help. I sent out a broadcast message to any god willing to answer my plea.

"Please!" I faced east and knelt. I brought my palms together and closed my eyes. I prayed with every cell of my being. "If you can hear me... never," I stretched my hands forward and faced my palms to the sky. I buried my face in the floor as I continued, "ever... cast my son as the lead in this drama." I rested there, my forehead on the floor, for a long time.

As peace began to trickle in, I continued to pray, "If you could give me one more little thing, I'd like to stick around long enough to raise him — my son — Ethan I mean. I'd really appreciate it. I know I sound selfish, but I really want to stay. At least think about it, okay? Thanks."

I didn't know what else to say: yet, in the hopes of aid from some compassionate god, I wordlessly poured my grief out onto the carpeting. My heart and my tears communicated what no words could convey. Eventually, drained and weary, I rolled onto my side and curled up into a ball. I hugged my knees and rocked myself while I tried to decide what to do.

Eventually, I decided on surgery, although with a surgeon other than the wolf-man. On the day before my forty-third birthday, an artist with a scalpel removed a portion of my breast, twenty-three lymph nodes and most, but not all of the cancer from my body.

## CHAPTER 6

# EDNA JUNE

Determined to learn how to live, I embarked on a journey of self-discovery — the meaning of life — the grand awakening. I felt compelled to go speeding off into the stratosphere, but my wheels were rusty. Instead I puttered slowly around the block a few times. I lost traction, slipped backward through my life and disappeared down the rabbit hole.

I lay in a heap at the bottom, the wind knocked out of me. As my eyes adjusted to the darkness, I could just make out the silhouette of an oddly familiar creature lurking in the corner. Sharp angles and elbows protruded in every direction from her rotund body. As she moved in closer, I noticed she wore dark-framed, cat-eye glasses.

She darted toward me. She didn't stop until she was nearly on top of me. For a moment she hovered there menacingly.

"Do you know who I am?" she asked as she turned her head sideways and peered over her glasses.

"I don't think so." I flinched. "Have we met before?"

"You may call me Edna, Edna June," she said and bowed slightly.

Before I had a chance to react, she leapt on top of me and seized me by the throat. She squeezed hard. My windpipe crackled under the pressure. I couldn't breathe.

She dragged me into a cage and locked the door behind us. She then lifted me to a standing position and quickly stripped me down. I glanced at my naked body surprised at the assortment of bandages still covering much of my carcass.

"What in the heck is going on here?" I said.

"So, you think you have the strength to fight me?" she taunted.

"Hyaa!" If it was a fight she wanted, a fight she would get. I raised my fists to defend myself.

Although I had an edge on Edna June in size, she had four times as many arms. She distracted me with a left jab, then reached in from the right and ripped a Band-Aid from my body.

"Ouwaa!" I cried out in pain. "Shit, woman!" I looked down to see how much skin I'd lost in the struggle. To my horror, puss and parasites swung from my pale, pasty flesh.

I froze, mortified. Then I screamed and clawed. "Get 'em off! Get 'em off!" I let down my guard.

Edna swooped in and savagely ripped and slashed at all of my tidy bandages. Emotional, physical, mental, spiritual hurts — it didn't matter. She exposed them all.

"Do you really think you are strong enough to fight me? You can still give up. You're good at giving up," she harassed, as she revealed every wound I had ever covered up and forgotten in my life.

The bandages had served as protection, but also as camouflage. Many of them had been there for years.

She dragged me over to a full-length mirror once again nearly crushing my windpipe. She jammed my face up against the glass.

"Look at you!" she ordered. Her nose wrinkled.

Under all of those bandages things had started to break down, to smell, to spread. No one could see it, but it was happening.

I had no idea the shape I was in. If I was hurt, I put a pretty Band-aid over it and forgot about it. In trying to protect myself, spare my feelings or those of others, I covered them all up and pretended they didn't exist anymore. I never really dealt with them. I never fully healed.

If one started to ooze out of the bandage, I just put on a bigger patch. I'd been doing this for years. Through neglect and denial, the wounds festered with resentment, hard feelings, self pity, even self-loathing. Now, I had a real mess on my hands. I slumped down onto the floor.

All my life I wanted to be right, to appear strong — like I had it together. I wanted to spare myself and others from the sting or ugliness of how I truly felt. In burying the hatchet in my own flesh, I didn't heal. The hidden wounds mushroomed in the moist darkness. The pain lingered. The poison quietly spread into other parts of my being.

*PU I stink!* I shuddered. My damp, grayish skin roiled and boiled, oozed and bubbled. A foul, yellowish liquid seeped from many of the infected eruptions. In some areas, parasites quietly fed. As I lay my head down on the cool mat, my skin rippled from the unfamiliarity of air. *I think I'm going to be sick,* I said to myself.

Scared and ashamed, I remained on the floor for hours. I secretly hoped and prayed that this was all just a bad dream; that I would wake-up to find this wasn't happening, but I'd run out of options. It was happening.

Edna stood over me. "That-a-girl," she mocked. "Give up."

"I won't," I whispered although I still couldn't find the strength to stand.

"Hmmm, who would have guessed that you would actually prove to be a worthy adversary after all? Clean yourself up!" Edna ordered, as she tossed me two knit hats (one white and one pink), and seven men's, white, Fruit-of-the-Loom, v-neck t-shirts. "This will be your sparring uniform for the next nine months."

I did as I was told.

Edna's voice quieted. "Do you know who I am now?" she asked

me again.

"What?" I replied despondently as I rested my back against the full-length mirror. "Truly, I don't give a crap about your name."

"Since we're talking life and death here, you should know who you're up against. Don't you think?"

I had to admit she got my attention.

She shook her head in disappointment. "You really don't know who I am, do you? Think!" she urged.

I eyed Edna for a long time. I swallowed hard. *Well, how many talking creatures have I met in my life with so many arms and legs?* I asked myself. I was pretty sure I knew who she was. She had to be cancer I surmised. But, oh, how I hoped I was wrong.

"Are you Cancer?" I asked pensively.

"In the flesh," she replied.

She'd grown stronger. I doubted I could take her. I considered giving up.

From the far corner, just outside the cage, Ethan, my eight-year-old-son; my husband, Gary; and my mom cheered me on. I considered my options. "I'm not going down that easily," I told her.

I turned and gazed into the mirror. I couldn't endure my own reflection. I didn't want the world to see me for who I was — vulnerable, wounded and weak, but Edna couldn't have cared less about my image. Life and death were her only concerns. I stood up. I faced myself then I faced her.

She smiled. She was a hard one to peg. I thought she'd come to kill me, and yet, she'd actually helped me. She'd given me the will and the tools to fight her. Maybe not out of kindness, maybe it's just what she does. Cancer lays the soul bare. I knew honesty would be the first step to healing. No more pretending. No more role-playing.

Once standing, the air seemed too thin to breathe. My knees wobbled, and I passed out. I awoke in a fetal position on the floor.

"Breathe!" Edna commanded. She spoke to my blisters and boils, my lesions and abscesses. To me she had nothing more to say.

I began to understand that bandages should be a temporary fix. For a little while, you can wrap up a hurt. It's even okay to sometimes go overboard with the bandages for the sympathy factor. I found out first-hand, if you don't expose your wounds and allow them breath, things start to break down and turn all smelly. Undetected, things deteriorate — spoiling what was once perfectly healthy. Maybe you can't see it. Maybe you covered it up with an adorable Hello Kitty Band-Aid. Nonetheless, it's happening.

I slowly realized that confronting the truth, although initially more painful, left me feeling cleansed and able to get on with life. I discovered that healing starts with forgiveness. I discovered that forgiveness starts with honesty. I discovered that, first and foremost, I had to be honest with myself.

I'm here to urge each and every one of you — take off the Band-Aids. Air out your wounds — the earlier the better. I know it's scary. I know it hurts. Rip them quickly. It stings more, but the pain doesn't last.

*If you would be a real seeker after truth, it is
necessary that at least once in your life you doubt,
as far as possible, all things.*

———— Descartes

CHAPTER 7

# SHOOT

Once Edna finished with my body she gathered up all the boundaries, rules and defining attributes of my tidy life — all the cultural, moral and religious fences I'd erected as a refuge. She lined them up like sitting ducks at a penny arcade. She handed me a gun. Since I'm no expert on guns, I really couldn't tell you what kind. Suffice it to say, a long gun with a wide barrel, a wooden stock and one hell of a kick.

"Shoot!" she commanded.

"No." I placed the gun on a high, worn-out, wooden farm table and crossed my arms.

"Where you see shelter and sanctuary I see a restrictive existence. If you want to leave here alive, you'll have to shoot your way out."

I had worked my entire life constructing these borders. They were all I had to keep fear at bay. Still, the desire to live drove me to pick up the gun. I leaned over the farm table. I took aim. I fired. Tears streamed down my cheeks. Rage replaced fear. Inwardly, I shouted, *I am the great destroyer!* Outwardly a wordless primordial war cry rose from my belly. I blasted, fast and hot. Pang! Pang! Tears continued to fall. I seethed with hatred at myself, my lot, my parents, my genes, my God. This life I'd so neatly sewn myself into exploded. The pieces became as dust, worthless — no — less than worthless.

"Die!" I screamed from deep within my soul. "Die! Die! Die!" I uttered with each blast. I emptied the gun. I continued to squeeze the trigger. "Die! Die! Die!" I gazed at the carnage before me. Initially satisfaction and strength filled my lungs as I heaved in and out. Then — nothing.

Edna gently took the gun from my hands. Did I see a flash of compassion or was it gratification in her eye? It didn't matter.

In the end I was left trembling. I no longer recognized myself or my life. Nothing mattered. *It's all dead to me anyway. I feel like crap.* I cursed at my life. I cared about nothing and no one. Enervated and unprotected, I backed myself into a dark cave and vowed to scratch the eyeballs out of anyone who dared come near. *Don't try to love me. I'm unlovable. Don't feel sorry for me. I've brought this on myself. Just — don't.* And with that, naked and dirty, I curled up in the dark, like a wounded badger, next to the ashes of my life and snarled at the light.

*If I were to wish for anything, I should not wish for wealth and power, but for the passionate sense of potential-for the eye which, ever young and ardent, sees the possible. Pleasure disappoints; possibility never.*

——————— Kierkegaard

CHAPTER 8

# P WORDS

My life, once packaged so neatly, smoldered in a heap of rubble. I felt lost and strange ...

The sun peeked cautiously over the horizon as though even Dawn feared the wrath of my reckless hatred. "I'm out of bullets," I conceded.

Bolstered by this tidbit of information, the sun rose a bit higher. With considerable trepidation, tiny rays of light trickled into my lair. I glowered and shrunk back into the darkness.

As the trickle of light became a stream, a swarm of P's moved toward me. Into the void of destruction the P's flew in and nursed my wounds. Perhaps, Possibly, Plausible, Potentially, Passable even Perchance, but positively nothing more definitive than Probably cleansed and consoled me. I have to admit I liked Probably the best.

Once upon a time I had all the answers. I knew definitively where I stood on any given issue. Black or white. Yes or no. I liked it that way. No room for contemplation. No compromise. I just knew — everything. Now I know nothing.

With time I began to embrace the nuances of living in gray. No longer sure of anything, I understood I didn't need to be. I zoomed around changing my degree of possibility and probability practically day by day, hour by hour. After all, it was my prerogative and I liked it.

CHAPTER 9

## TASTE THE TAILS

Edna June returned. Over her right shoulder she carried her doctor's bag. She flung it into my badger hole and climbed in behind it.

"You've done well. Better your borders, your restrictions, your limitations and your margins, than your life," she said.

"You're pretty strong," I muttered as I glanced in her general direction.

"Strength is what you need," she answered as she tended to some of my bigger wounds.

"Why are you helping me?" I asked.

"I prefer an opponent to a victim," she answered. You chose to fight. You stood up to me. You stood up for yourself. I like that and because of that, I will help you live to fight another day. "

"Remember back in the summer of '95 when you and Gary took the Snowman out for an afternoon of crawdad fishing?" Edna asked as she continued to tend my wounds.

"Yeah," I answered.

I remembered that summer well. The Snowman was sick; my bones knew it even though my brain had no idea.

That particular afternoon, for old time's sake, we planned a fishing expedition. Instead of fish, we planned to hunt for crayfish. Southerners eat those things. We decided to give them a try.

My grandma saved everything. We poked around her closets and found a couple of metal coat hangers which we formed into circles. We wove old onion bags, in and out, around the circular coat hangers to form fishing nets.

Onion nets in hand, my husband, the Snowman and I set out for the banks of a cool, shallow brook in search of the illusive crayfish. Gary and I discovered, early on, that crayfish move really fast in reverse. If we quietly placed our nets behind one and scared him from the front, he would practically jump backward into the net. I caught thirty or so. My husband caught about the same. With a lot of help and a pinch of mercy, the Snowman caught *one*, scrawny crayfish.

When we got back to Grandma and Grandpa's, no one felt much like eating those dirty, little buggers. So I boiled them up with some sea salt and Old Bay seasoning, just until they turned bright red. After plunging them in ice water I picked the tails clean and discarded the heads and bodies. I packed the tails in fresh water and threw them in the freezer for another day.

"I was there you know. I was with him," Edna said pulling me back from the memory.

"Huh?" *Was this Cancer's attempt at small talk?* I wondered. Of course I knew she was there. Perhaps I didn't want to admit it at the time, but I knew. How could I not know? The Snowman died less than six months later. Of, what was it? Oh yeah, it was cancer!

I didn't feel much like chatting. Certainly not with that snowman killer. I looked at her. "Um, yeah," I replied, secretly hoping she'd shut-up and tend to my wounds.

"Why did you freeze the tails?" she asked.

"Because nobody really felt like eating them, and we figured we could eat them a different day."

"The Snowman knew he'd never taste the tails. It wasn't important to him. In fact, he hadn't gone along to fish at all. He was soaking up valuable time. He already knew his days were numbered."

"When you near the end of your life, time gets all mixed up," Edna continued. "As the Snowman and I sat in the shade, we saw you as a five-year-old girl splashing through the shallows in your rubber boots and calico sundress. Together, we watched contentedly as you ensnared water bugs, frogs, minnows and crayfish. Even now you grab hold of everything in your sight. By contrast, the Snowman blissfully plucked one more precious memory for his vase."

"I understand," I replied.

"Do you?"

"I think I do."

Often we are so caught up in doing and becoming, that we miss the real riches in life. That summer the Snowman celebrated afternoon. He celebrated togetherness. I put my big catch of crayfish tails in the freezer; the Snowman carried his one more memory with him forever. Which one of us was a more successful fisherman that afternoon?

I couldn't see that then. Only when Cancer sat with me, did I understand why a dying snowman had no desire to catch crayfish.

I closed my eyes and listened intently to the sounds of my life. I breathed in the soft scent of my home, my world, my family.

"Thank you for the memory and for the lesson, Edna, but I'm going to fight you anyway."

"I was hoping you'd say that," she replied. "I enjoy a good fight. Now, get some rest, you're going to need it."

In the months that followed, Edna would become my coach, my sparring partner, my nursemaid and my arch nemesis. In her own raw-boned, tough and emotionless way, she could bend any cell in my body to her will. She had a purpose. Her task was to get me to move forward or die. Retreat was out of the question.

*If you are losing a tug-of-war with a tiger,*
*give him the rope before he gets to your arm.*
*You can always buy a new rope*

——— Max Gunther

CHAPTER 10

# MY JOURNEY BEGINS

Two weeks later I met with the oncologist. A young nurse, pregnant with twins, showed me to an examining room. As she took my vitals we joked lightheartedly that she should name the twins she was carrying Rascal One and Rascal Two. I felt optimistic and confident. I assured myself the worst was over.

Five or ten minutes later a small brownish man with a kind face and a brown suit entered the examining room. He spoke in a soft, sing-song voice that immediately put me at ease. As we talked, he faced me, but his eyes remained closed. "How much information would you like?" he asked politely.

I furrowed my brow. *That's an odd question,* I thought. I hesitated. "All of it?" I answered indecisively. "Is there really any other option?"

The oncologist smiled pleasantly but averted my question. Instead, he began typing on the computer. He occasionally murmured something about various markers. He asked me a few questions then left the room. Moments later he returned with a printout. I smiled and took the paper from him. The paper contained a simple black and white probability graph of my life. Medically speaking, the graph indicated that, if I did no more doctoring, I had a ninety-eight percent chance that I would succumb to cancer within ten years. There was a one percent chance I could die of something else. Perhaps I could get hit by a bus. Not much chance of that though.

I was left with a one percent chance to be alive and cancer free.

I immediately pictured my son. I had waited thirty-five years to become a mom. (Best job I ever had.) As Ethan frolicked through the hallways of his elementary school, a man I met only moments before tried to hand me my pink slip. No, No, No, No, No! I planted my feet and clenched my fists.

*I want... I want...* I began talking to myself. *What do I want? More than anything I want my son to remember me!* Even if I can't stay long enough to see him off to college, I want to live long enough for him to recall our time together. Kids are so resilient. But, I'm not.

I needed time. I felt like a contestant on the Wheel of Fortune. "I'd like to buy some time, Doc."

I chose full, head-on assault. "Hit me with everything you've got." The way I figured it, each day I bought gave me time to find the answers I sought. Each day gave my son time to age and therefore to remember how much I love him. Each day I spent looking over my shoulder for death to arrive gave me a few more moments to embrace life. As my head filled and spilled with matters I never previously contemplated, it suddenly became very important to collect memories. I had wasted so much of my life. *I can't die!* I reminded myself. *I haven't even lived yet!*

The oncologist and I, through strong negotiations, hammered out a plan. I wanted a minimum of two years. Together we mapped out a conventionally prescribed route, but at high speed.

Now was the time for action. We needed to be aggressive. I believe each person should choose the avenue that fits his or her personality and situation best. For me, this high-speed conventional approach just felt right.

I knew my doctors would not let go of me until I was cancer-free for the moment. Whether I would remain cancer-free was iffy. I chose to let modern, medicine deal with the immediate threat while I worked on long-term health. I had some prep work to do, some stumbling to do, some falling flat on my face to do. I worked on collecting memories and turning my life around. That shouldn't take two years, I hoped. But, I know myself. I take baby steps. I feel sorry for myself. I fall back into habits that no longer serve me. I don't work well under pressure. Believing I had at least two years breathing room comforted me.

I've always felt that disease stemmed from "dis ease" — an uneasiness or unhappiness that begins in the mind or possibly the soul. Interestingly enough, my theory remained the same as I faced my own disease. All too often theories apply to somebody else but, when faced with a personal challenge, all those preconceived notions fly out the window.

I had a time in my life when I was unhappy — shaken to the core. I had defined myself as a wife and a mother. As that world crumbled I didn't know who I was or where I fit in. I put on a brave face and pretended that nothing was wrong. The "dis-ease" grew undetected below the surface. That was four years before I finally sat in the oncologist's office and chose to cope with my "dis-ease". During that time a big, yet manageable loss became stage three cancer.

Now I had to tackle some tough questions. I opted to fill those initial days with soul-searching and change. *What did it all mean to me? If my days were numbered, what did I want to do with the rest of my life? Who did I want to be remembered as?* Eventually, I came up with a roadmap.

Phase One - Planning my journey: I chose to be completely honest with myself as I answered the following questions to the best of my ability.
Who am I?
Where am I at?

<u>Phase Two – Choosing a destination:</u> I chose to throw fear and reputation to the wind as I answered two more questions.

Who *could* I be?

What do I *want* to do?

<u>Phase Three: My journey begins:</u> I took complete responsibility for the mess I had gotten myself into and I made a promise.

I would take at least one step in the right direction every day.

Even if I resorted to crawling an inch on my hands and knees I would commend myself for the effort.

<u>Phase Four: My journey comes full circle:</u> Although I had no idea how to accomplish my goals I would initiate a course and move forward.

I would honor my spirit for a valiant attempt regardless of the outcome.

I would be happy regardless of the circumstances.


"I warned you that it's going to be tough," Edna said.

"And I promised you that I would fight," I answered.

I had watched the Snowman battle for twenty years before his final surrender. I knew I was in for the fight of my life.

## Chapter 11

# Death of a Snowman

Six months after our onion-net crawdad-hunting expedition, the Snowman lay in a hospital bed weak, out of breath and withered by cancer. He had come to the end of his life. The doctors had done all they could. It was just a matter of time.

For twenty years we had waited for Death to arrive. Now he stood patiently in the doorway. The Snowman knew it and I knew it. "I have to go home," he reminded me.

"Not yet," I replied. I turned so he couldn't see the tears welling up in my eyes.

I needed to collect just a few more memories. He had so many things left to teach me. Who would I turn to when I had one of those questions that only a dad can answer? *Please, no, he can't go — not yet. Please God, don't take him,* I silently prayed.

"Remember all those people who cried at my hospital bed twenty years ago?" The Snowman's voice pulled me from my prayer. "Remember how they pitied me?" As he said the word pity a dark cloud passed through his face. The darkness was palpable still it would take me many years to understand.

"Yeah," I responded numbly.

"Well, I've outlived half of them," he concluded. He seemed satisfied or, at the very least, content to be at the end of his life. I clung to the only thread that held him in this world — his love for me. He could have easily severed the line and passed through to the other side, but he waited for me to willingly let go. Letting go would be one of the hardest and yet most beautiful choices I'd have to make in my life.

Call it what you will, but I kept him in here for one more week. I needed the time to properly say good-bye. I needed the time to feel the warmth of his hand in mine. I needed to comb his hair like I had when I was a child and to tell him how much I would miss him.

I knew he couldn't breathe. I knew that when he couldn't catch his breath, fear and panic set in. I knew he suffered, and still, I couldn't let him go.

*Soon,* I told myself, *but not today.*

The Snowman leaned forward and grasped my hand. "This is important," he said. He took off his oxygen mask and began to whisper. "**All** that really matters in life is that you are truly happy. Are you happy?" he asked.

As all the reasons raced across my mind as to why now, of all times, I was incapable of happiness, I shook my head "yes" — and "no". *How could I be happy?* I thought. *I can't stand to see him suffer, yet I can't bear to let him go.*

"Only you can make you happy." Exhausted from the effort it took to speak, the Snowman lay his head back, replaced his oxygen mask and closed his eyes.

At the time, I didn't know how to reply to his plea for my happiness. I simply let the conversation drop. The last thing I wanted to do was hurt his feelings. After all, this was his finale, the culminating wisdom of an entire lifetime. His words seemed beside-the-point and unimportant. It would take me thirteen years to realize how wrong I was.

That's how our week went. I continued to keep the Snowman

in this world against his will. He didn't complain. I'm not sure if he was really that patient with me or if speaking was so difficult that he just chose not to. Either way, I reclined in my chair and cherished the warmth of his hand.

On the sixth night the nurse woke me; something was wrong. The snowman's hand had slipped from mine. I jumped from my chair. I grabbed his hand and placed his palm to my heart. I leaned over the bed until our noses collided.

"No!" I pleaded with him. I stared frantically into his closed eyes. I squeezed his hand tightly against my chest hoping he could feel my heart breaking.

Finally he opened his eyes. He smiled a sad, sheepish smile filled with pain and love.

I studied his face for many moments. I wanted to remember every crease in his forehead, the pale blue of his eyes, the way his eyebrows made S curves when he worried.

I laced his fingers tightly in mine. I knew this would be our last night. As the snow began to softly fall outside, inside I wordlessly made a promise to a Snowman to set him free.

*He who doesn't lose his wits over certain things has no wits to lose.*

———— Emilia Galotti

CHAPTER 12

## LIBERTY BELLS AND MARBLES

The time had come to keep my promise — the time for letting go.

In the morning the Snowman appeared revived. He had an appetite and an energy level I hadn't seen in him since I arrived seven horribly wonderful days ago.

I took advantage of his high spirits for a deathbed confession. "Remember Liberty Bell?" I began. Liberty Bell was the Snowman's prized, purebred, Saanens dairy goat. He bought her from a commune tucked way back in the Kettle Moraine in 1976.

He nodded, "yes."

"Well," I continued, "I went to the farm one day to do the chores. Liberty Bell was in labor. One kid lay on the ground next to her. He was fine. She had the back legs of the second kid sticking out.

"You know — there." I pointed between my legs in case he wasn't at all certain where babies come from.

"Well, I didn't know what to do. After all, I was just a kid myself."

As I continued to relay the story my words picked up speed. "I thought the baby might still be alive, so I pulled. At first nothing happened, so I pulled harder. The baby slid out. She was already dead – probably suffocated. Then Liberty Bell collapsed in the straw and stopped breathing. I know all this happened a long time ago. I probably should have told you sooner." Having finally gotten the weight of that secret off my chest, I sat back and relaxed.

"Anyway, I just thought you should know." I shrugged as my words came to a screeching halt and lay in a tangled heap in the Snowman's lap. I breathed a solid sigh of relief.

The Snowman sat bolt-upright his face red with anger. "You **killed** my goat?"

His reaction surprised and delighted me. I was seeking death-bed forgiveness for a secret I had harbored for nearly two decades. I got something much more valuable. I got a glimpse of an old, fiery Snowman. The same old Snowman I knew and loved; a moment to treasure for years to come; and the strength to say good-bye.

Later that day, I held his hand like I had done so many times before. I bent down and gently kissed his face. I stood and walked slowly toward the door. As his soul left his body it shot through me like an arrow. Half of my guts and all of my marbles drained out in a heavy stream. I lost my footing. I staggered and I waited.

The Snowman's chest rose then fell, each inhale weaker than the last. It was like watching a ball that had been dropped. His breaths continued to come slower and slower until... nothing. I waited in anticipation for the next breath. It never came. He had gone. I immediately wanted him back.

At his funeral, we served cold crayfish pizza. The tails he never tasted.

*Happiness is beneficial for the body but it is grief that develops the powers of the mind.*

───── Marcel Proust

CHAPTER 13

# GOOD GRIEF

G rief cleaved me open, ripped a gaping hole in my marble bag and spilled my marbles all out into full view. Instead of quickly gathering them up and pushing on, I decided to analyze each one. Oh, it's not for the faint of heart. I had become a sappy puddle even to myself. All my baggage lay strewn about before me. I didn't care. I picked up the first marble. As I turned it in my hand I asked myself, *do I really want to keep this one?*

I heard whispers: "Put her on some medicine. Get her some help."

"No," I whispered in return. If I chose to swallow a pill, I would also swallow my feelings. Death isn't simple, and I needed time to come to terms with it and to understand how I felt and why I felt the way I did. In order to heal, I needed to walk the labyrinth of grief and to ultimately discover peace.

Through the grief of that first year, I learned that emotional anguish causes physical pain and despair causes illness. I contracted pneumonia. I couldn't breathe. In the end, I'd watched the Snowman fight for every breath he took. Was my subsequent inability to breathe sympathy, empathy, illness or grief? I don't know. I just kept walking.

Slowly I released the anger, the misery, the regrets and despair. One by one I dropped them into the labyrinth. I recalled the Snowman's dying words, "All that really matters in this world is that you're happy." I found little flecks of happiness and I collected them. They became visible to me in the dark labyrinth of grief. I hadn't noticed them in the light.

In time, contentment and ease, peace and happiness replaced the sorrow. Walking healed me. In time, I could finally remember the Snowman with happiness in my heart for having known and loved him instead of pain at the loss. Grief taught me to let go of what was. Only then could I make room in my life for what is and for what could be.

*Either move or be moved.*

———— Ezra Pound

CHAPTER 14

# GREEK TAKE-OUT

I heard a persistent knock on the door. I peeked out of my front window. On the other side of the door stood a strange, mesmerizingly handsome man in an Egyptian cotton tunic with a Nehru collar. He leaned on an elaborately carved, gilded walking stick. His dishwater blonde hair curled tightly around his face and temples. My heart fluttered. I have to admit, I was scared. "Go away. I don't need your help." I called through the closed door.

"But you asked for it," he answered.

"I changed my mind," I announced coldly.

As I peered through the peephole I watched him smile warmly. That did nothing to calm my nerves. Even without his traditional winged hat and shoes I recognized him immediately. Hermes, the Greek god of travelers and shepherds, merchants and thieves stood just beyond the door, and he called me out.

In college I may have gotten a B- in Greek mythology, but I remembered that Hermes was *Psychopomp*, guide of the dead. I really wasn't looking for a tour of Hades, since that's usually a one-way trip.

"Go away!" I tried to persuade him to leave one last time, but he wasn't taking "No" for an answer.

Contemplating my options, I stood frozen with my back to the door. I had asked for help; this was true. I had sent out a broadcast message. I knew I had prayed to all gods, to any god. Still I hoped for *(I don't know)* something or somebody different, somebody else, somebody less scary.

*I'm a Lutheran for God's sake!*

Now that he was here, was I willing to take what I could get?

Hermes waited patiently. He wasn't leaving without me. I slowly opened the door. As the sun glowed orange along the western horizon, I stepped across the threshold to begin my journey.

"Got your ready bag?" Hermes asked.

I knew I didn't have one.

He must have deduced as much by the look on my face. "It's okay. I'll help you pack later. Let's go."

We stood for a moment together on the front porch. Hermes stroked his hairless chin. "Let's see, before we begin, you must stop," he said as he leaned forward and looked into my eyes. "Stop performing and start living."

"What?" I stumbled back from the power of his gaze.

"You are so busy fulfilling roles that you've forgotten why you came here. You need to stop it."

"People are counting on me, Hermes. Paha, stop fulfilling roles, that's a luxury I don't have," I countered as I placed my hands on my hips and glared back at him.

"Are you really so important?" He didn't wait for a reply. He turned and began to walk.

For a moment I considered just standing there and letting him walk away without me, but I knew I needed his help. I jogged to catch up.

"Do you honestly think that other people's lives will not go on without you? We are all replaceable. The magic of you lies in who you are, not in what you do for others. And to discover who you are, we will have to get rid of this." He pointed at me. "Just for the time being, "he added and patted my forearm.

"What this?" I asked.

"This, this," he reiterated sweeping both hands the full length of my body.

"You mean my body?" I began. "No! Oh, come on Hermes, we just got back together, my body and I. Don't make me leave it already," I pleaded.

"Trust me, it's for you own good," he stated impassively.

"Are you sure?" I asked one more time in an attempt to keep it together.

"Entirely," he threw back.

"If you're certain, I know just the place. Could we make a small detour?" I asked.

"Sure," he replied.

We continued on in silence toward the oncologist's office. Once there I unceremoniously dropped off my body.

"Good choice," Hermes remarked.

As we walked along, I considered my life and the roles I played. I lived most moments like a pawn on a chessboard. For the comfort and growth of others I'd willingly allowed myself to be attracted, repelled and manipulated, even sacrificed.

Perhaps I was more concerned than I realized that, just maybe, I am loved only for what services I offer. If I stopped performing, would everyone go away? If I stopped helping everyone else, would I be all alone?

As I contemplated my vast fear of loneliness, we entered a locker room. The stale scent of sweaty gym socks filled the air. "Now you must undress," Hermes ordered.

"Undress? I just left my body back at the oncologist's office. What more could you possibly want me to leave behind?" I puzzled.

"Your intellect. This is not a civilized journey. You will have to leave reason here."

Too sick and tired to argue, I sat down on a wooden bench and did as I was told. I methodically stepped out of my mind. I neatly folded it and placed it in my lap as I examined the row of gun-metal gray lockers that stretched out before me. I opened the door to locker number 79. Inside hung an unbleached muslin gown and a well-worn pair of leather wrestling boots. I placed my neatly folded mind on the top shelf of the locker. I slipped on the muslin gown and sat back down on the wooden bench. I placed my feet into the mid-calf-high boots and drew the laces up tightly. They fit more like socks with soles than boots. I stood and marched in place admiring the exquisite fit and feel of my new boots. "Hmmm, snug. Can I keep them?" I asked Hermes.

He didn't reply.

After glancing once more inside the locker, I lifted the latch and silently closed the door. I stood with my face jammed tightly against the cold metal. *Bookends to infinity*, I told myself, hoping that I could somehow remember where I'd left my mind once it was gone.

Feeling vulnerable and wild, I pressed hard against the locker door. I begged my mind to ooze through the louvers and seep back into place. My ears twitched and my eyes darted. I'd now let both my body and mind go. I feared I would slowly disappear. Instead, to my amazement, I still existed.

A sense of calm descended upon me, and I felt intuitive perhaps even wise. Yes. I felt wise in a way much bigger than myself. Instinct controlled what had once been adulterated.

"It's time to go." Hermes reached for my hand and my elbow. He guided me away from the lockers. While I readied myself for the journey, the sun sank low behind the horizon. Darkness had set in – a darkness as black as coal. My skin prickled in fear and anticipation. I looked over at Hermes for reassurance and for the first time I realized that we had met before. Where did I know him from?

I stopped walking and stared at Hermes in amazement. "I

remember," I whispered.

He just smiled. I reached over and grasped his hand. We walked along in silence. As we descended into a steep ravine, I reminisced about our first meeting so long ago. I didn't know his name at the time.

*Intellect is to emotion as our clothes are to our bodies:  we could not very well have a civilized life without clothes, but we would be in a poor way if we had only clothes without bodies*

———— Alfred North Whitehead

CHAPTER 15

# FROM HERMES TO ETERNITY

M any years ago, during one of my darkest hours, a man came to me. I didn't know him, but I trusted him. He took my hand. He wanted to walk. I felt safe in his presence.

Together we moved silently through the darkness. Eventually we arrived high atop a rocky outcropping. A beautiful tapestry of light sprawled across the valley floor below us. I was reminded of looking down on a city at night from an airplane. The view this night was considerably more beautiful.

A din filled the valley. Noise. Not voices, but sound. The sound of light. The fabric of light lived and breathed. Some areas of the tapestry had no light. As I wondered if the lights had burnt out or where just missing in those areas, a silence descended like a blanket. It became so quiet I froze and held my breath.

The lights which had before been blinking like Christmas in the suburbs, now also became motionless. We waited in anticipation, although, I have to confess, I didn't know what for. The man standing behind me grabbed my wrists and wrapped my arms around me like a strait jacket. He firmly grasped my elbows and squeezed. Neither of us moved. I felt confused yet safe in his strong embrace.

"Here he comes," the stranger whispered. A blinding white light cut through the darkness. As it reached high above us, it exploded into the full spectrum of color and light. A rainbow made up of millions of individual points of light hovered for a moment overhead. In unison the rainbow of lights flipped over, arched in the opposite direction and dove gracefully down toward the fabric of lights below.

The awaiting tapestry began to dance, whirl, and cheer. I watched in awe as the individual points of colored light slowly fell. Each drifted effortlessly into a dark space in the weave. Somehow I knew that the bright, white beam of light was the Snowman.

The fabric knew he was coming and eagerly awaited his arrival. In preparation, a magnificent void had been purposefully woven into the cloth – the cloth from which we are all cut and subsequently return. As the explosion of color and light came to rest, the void glowed with the accumulated colors of his lifetime.

Neither the stranger nor I spoke again, but inside I could hear a voice: "I have prepared a place for you." The place had been set and, as the tapestry became fulfilled, it pulsated with joy. How patiently the lights had waited. How they celebrated his coming. How selfish I had been to want to keep him here.

*The secret for harvesting from existence
the greatest fruitfulness and greatest
enjoyment is-to live dangerously.*

——— Nietzsche

How many gardens in this world of ours
Hold blossoms that have never come to flowers?
A sudden wind comes coldly by —
The rose tree bids its fairest bud good-bye
How many ships of ours go out to sea
In search of heavens that shall tranquil be?
The storms of fate their fairest hopes o'er set,
And there is naught to do except forget.
How many wear a smile upon their face
Although their hearts may hold an empty place?
None know the heights nor depths of their regrets,
But God remembers when the world forgets.

———— Clifton Bingham

CHAPTER 16

# THE GARDEN

Hermes handed me an apple — a Honey Crisp — my favorite. The gesture pulled me from my memories. He slapped me on the back as if to say, "welcome back."

"We've met before," I said in astonishment.

Hermes just smiled. He rubbed his apple on the front of his teacloth tunic and motioned for me to follow him.

I too smiled as I once again jogged to keep up. Hermes may very well be the angel of death; still I was beginning to enjoy his company. And let's face it he was not only beautiful to look at he had great style.

The unadorned tunic draped gracefully across his athletic frame. He wore wide-legged pants and sandals. *Beautiful! Adonis has nothing on him.* I sunk my teeth deep into the apple. Juice filled my mouth as my stomach noisily declared gastronomic approval.

Hermes finished his apple first. All that remained were seven seeds and the stem. He bent low and delicately released them on the rolling Wisconsin grassland. I'd grown up less than fifteen miles from here and stood in marvel at the lush open savannah sprinkled with ancient, gnarled oak trees. I could picture large game coming over the rise to munch lazily upon the vegetation. The land lay wide and dry, yet not a prairie. The landscape rose and fell. Giant trees offered shade and sanctuary. The view resembled a picture I'd seen in National Geographic of South Africa more than the Wisconsin of my youth.

"If you were a plant, what do you think you would be?" Hermes asked as he glanced rather disappointedly at the fat, browning apple core I still carried.

"I don't know. I never gave it much thought," I replied.

"Well, do all plants thrive in lush soil? Do all flowers bloom in summer?"

"Huh?" I hadn't really been listening. I saw the way he looked at my apple core and was trying to rid myself of it without his knowing.

For the moment Hermes gave up this line of questioning and we walked along in silence. For that I was glad. Eventually we came upon a small gate flanked by cypress trees. As I looked around, Hermes unlocked the gate. We entered. "Meet your kinfolk, Mortality and Eternity." Hermes flashed me a broad smile as he motioned to the cypress trees on either side of us.

"What are you going on about? Plants again? Trees? Last I checked I'm a human." I no longer cared what he thought about my apple core and sent it high and arcing toward a patch of scrub-brush off to our left.

"The imposing cypress marks that place where an opening exists to the underworld. You may have noticed them in cemeteries," Hermes informed me.

Panic set in. How could he march me right up to the gates of hell? Just when I was beginning to trust him — to like him? I'd nearly forgotten that he was the guide to the underworld.

My breath caught in my throat as I tried to speak. "Hermes, I don't like it here. I want to leave," I muttered. I turned my back to him. With my fingertips I pressed my eyelids tightly to my eyes. *This isn't happening. Not already. Hermes is the guide to the underworld for dead souls. I'm not dead yet! Am I? I can't be.*

I sank to my knees and threw up a sort of yellowish, greenish foam on a jumble of undergrowth, rocks and thistles. It looked more like something that comes out of my dog. *If I eat some grass, will I feel better?* I wondered.

Hermes helped me to my feet and handed me his handkerchief. He gently caressed my forehead with the palms of his hands. I closed my eyes. I felt like a foolish child.

He then placed a gentle hand on the back of my shoulder. "Many people thrive only in a rich, stable environment. Others are better in less hospitable terrain. You seem to flourish in between. Without a doubt you are a cypress tree. "

My face flushed with embarrassment, then paled in panic, then flushed again — this time in anger. I couldn't sort out which emotion to settle on. They all pulled and tugged for top billing. I still wasn't entirely sure if I was alive or dead or soon to be dead. "Is that why you brought me here — to flourish?" I asked.

"Perhaps. That is up to you. Do you know where you are?"

"Ah... well," I began rather pensively, "if the cypress trees are any indication, five seconds from hell, I'd gather. And, by the way, I'm not going!" I sat down and crossed my arms over my chest.

Hermes erupted in deep, carefree laughter. "Relax."

"Relax? You brought me **here** and now you're telling me to relax?"

"Where is here?"

I looked around. We stood just inside the gates of a walled garden. Weeds overran the once-verdant landscape. In the garden's center stood a magnificent yew tree. It was ancient — four thousand years old. The tree had exposed roots and delicate, glimmering leaves. On the highest branch sat an eagle.

"We have come to harvest the bark of the yew," Hermes informed me. He then went on to explain that he intended to make a magical serum. He would eventually ask me to have this liquid administered directly into my veins.

"But the yew is poisonous." I protested.

"Only to man and other domestic animals," Hermes replied. "That's why you had to leave your mind and your body behind. The wild deer known as the hart is actually nourished by the yew," Hermes added in an attempt to reassure me, "as is the soul."

"I really don't want any part of this, Hermes," I protested. "I'm afraid."

"I know you are," he sympathized.

"I could die, Hermes!" My voice rose in pitch and volume.

"You might," he shrugged, "but if you don't do this, you surely will." He remained calm. He held my gaze for a long time before continuing, "Did you see the eagle sitting high up in the tree? She delicately holds a yew berry in her beak. Should the yew of this lifetime, that is to say the you of your current lifetime, die, she'll swallow the berry and fly off. The seed will pass unharmed through the eagle to again become a lifetime in another place in another time. All the knowledge and memories of the yew travel in the seed with the eagle," Hermes explained.

"Let me see if I can get this straight. You're telling me the yew is me — is my soul? "I don't want to live another lifetime. I want to live this one," I snapped.

"That's why we're here," he said as he tried to soothe me with his words. "And that's why I'm gathering the bark of the ancient yew. Only the yew that lives deep within you — only the purest essence of yew can heal you.

Is that somehow supposed to make me feel better? Look at this place," I shook my head as I threw my hands in the air. "It's a mess!"

"Now do you know where you are?" Hermes slowly asked. He emphasized each word.

"I'm not sure," I replied although I was beginning to understand. Still, I didn't like what I saw.

"I think you do."

I swallowed hard. "This, (I weakly waved my hand over the weed infested land) is my garden — my life." I surveyed the neglect and disarray. I felt defeated before I began, and I knew I couldn't fix it on my own. With resignation I conceded, "Hermes, I want to go ahead with the serum."

"Good," he replied as he surveyed my garden. "Yes. This is your garden and the time has come to tend it." Reflected in his eyes I glimpsed an underlying, although severely neglected, splendor.

On the back of my knee I sensed a tender rat-a-tap-tap. I turned to see a small, kindly, gray-haired garden gnome tugging persistently at my trousers. She resembled a dandelion that had gone to seed.

"She's here to prepare you for the elixir. Go with her." Hermes threw me a reassuring glance. He then began harvesting the bark of the yew. I stood dumbfounded. I didn't really want to go hang-out with Garden-gnome Granny. I didn't want to prepare for an elixir that might as easily kill me as cure me.

"Go!" He ordered.

The gnome wrapped her tiny hand around my index finger. She led me toward a small half-timber cottage. I ducked to pass through the doorway. Once inside she grabbed a pie tin filled with food scraps from a small, hand-carved table near the door and set it on the dirt floor. A family of raccoons scampered out from behind a sewing table and began to feast. Contentedly the tiny gnome wiped her hands briskly on her apron. She nodded at the raccoons, turned and firmly gripped the pinky and thumb of my left hand.

"My friends call me Flit," she informed me as she enthusiastically pumped my hand up and down. She released me, gripped the edges of her pale blue skirt and curtsied.

"Now, let's get down to business. You will lie" — she looked left, then right, then left, then right, as though she'd misplaced the sofa, before pointing directly in front of her — "there." She motioned toward a chaise lounge covered in plush, greenish-gray moss. She then wiped her hands once more on her apron. Her eyes darted around the one-room cabin. She gathered up the bottom of her skirt and apron, creating a fabric bowl. She then scurried around the house collecting items and placing them, one by one, into the folds of her skirts. Her load quickly grew and grew. She stood in the center of the room and spun one, two, three times.

"Yes. Good," she said, although I think she spoke more to herself than to me. "I believe I have everything. Now, go lie down."

Instead, I sat cautiously on the edge of the chaise lounge. Not wanting to crush the moss, I tried keeping most of my weight evenly distributed between the palms of my hands and the soles of my feet.

Flit swiftly unpacked her apron. Near the moss-covered lounger she placed a painting of Bird Parker's alto sax, a statue of the Buddha, a well-worn, leather-bound Bible, a tall, tapered candle, (red-and-white-striped like a candy cane), a worry stone (I remember thinking I might need a couple more of those), a box of Kleenex and three of my son's eyelashes in a Dixie cup.

"The eyelashes are in case you need to make a wish," Flit informed me as she smoothed the fabric of her skirt and apron down until it once again brushed neatly against her ankles.

"Let's go." She motioned for me to follow her as she hustled out of the front door and back toward Hermes.

Outside the sun shone so brightly it hurt my eyes. Everything gleamed and glistened. I couldn't see more than two feet in front of me. Finally my eyes adjusted. Hermes still knelt at the base of the great yew. He had nearly finished gathering bark from the tree. He didn't look up. "Tend your garden," he ordered.

I assessed my lot. A few seeds I'd planted. Most blew in on a breeze. For years I'd left my garden fallow and neglected.

"Where do I start?" I asked.

"Perhaps from the beginning or better yet from where you are." Hermes answered impatiently.

*What the hell does that mean?* I silently asked myself. I sat down at the edge of my garden and started to cry. I didn't even want to set foot in this place where nothing beautiful grew. Flit and Hermes left me alone. The two of them went back to Flit's house to extract the essence from the bark of the yew and ready the resulting liquid for my veins.

I stretched out and watched the few wispy clouds that hung low in the sky. I closed my eyes and fell asleep. I awoke to a tickle on my nose. I rubbed my nose and tried to go back to sleep. The tickle returned, more persistently this time. I opened my eyes. The sun rested on the horizon, bathing the world in a golden glow. I smiled at the sun then placed my hands behind my head. Above me fluttered a fairy all dressed in white. "Look at you!" I exclaimed. "Aren't you just adorable?"

The fairy placed a tiny finger to her lips. "Sh-h-h." She flew lower, close to my ear. "Ich heisse Swantje," she whispered.

"Did you say your name is Swantje? In German?" I asked. I had taken German in college and was pleased to finally get a chance to use it. "Guten Tag!" I replied perhaps a bit too enthusiastically.

"Yes. Guten Tag." she replied. Her tone implied that she hadn't come to offer me German lessons.

"I've traveled a very long way to see you. May I rest?" she asked.

"Of course," I offered. Unbeknownst to me, fairies don't stop flying until they ask politely if it's okay to land. I put out my index finger like a perch.

The beautiful fairy hovered for a second as she gathered the many layers of her gossamer skirt high above her knees. Sensible black shoes protruded from beneath the gauzy white frill of her gown. She kicked her feet straight out in front of her and plopped down hard, tush first. "Whew. Thanks." She shrugged and dangled her feet over the edge.

She unstrapped a large basket from her back. "I've brought you some things that may help you on your journey," she said as she brushed a bead of sweat and an unruly blonde lock from her forehead.

She produced an apple from the basket, "for health" she informed me as she gently replaced it. One by one she showed me the items from her basket. "One shamrock for luck, one mushroom to help you see what has always been there, and a heart filled with love. Keep your basket safe. I have to go."

"But you just got here," I protested.

She didn't reply. Instead she handed me the basket. In my hand it was no larger than a thimble. She awkwardly maneuvered her feet around until she rested on all fours. She abruptly stiffened her arms and legs and shot off backward from her perch. Mystified, I gazed in the direction of her flight. She hovered for a moment over a scrawny tree; then, as quickly as she had arrived, she was gone.

The malnourished tree stretched tall and narrow to escape the weeds. It seemed to sway gently from side to side as if to gain my attention.

Hermes walked over. "Do you recognize the tree? That one, there," he said as he pointed to the swaying tree.

"No."

"It's a myrtle. The tree of Aphrodite. The tree of love."

"Gary?" Stunned at my own neglect, I ran over and pulled frantically at the weeds that attempted to smother the half-starved tree, but there were too many of them. At his side, stooped low beneath the encroaching weeds, a second smaller tree fought for space. "And Ethan! Dear God, somebody help me!" I screamed, but I knew nobody could. I had to help myself.

I wildly ripped at the weeds that tried to smother these two miraculous myrtles — my family — my boys. My love for them gave me hope and determination.

Out of this love I knew what I had to do. I would protect my beautiful myrtles (as best as I could) and poison the entire weed patch every other week for sixteen weeks. I would then set the most overgrown spaces ablaze. Perhaps then, I could begin again — weed free.

*Words have no power to impress the mind*
*without the exquisite horror of their reality.*

———— Edgar Allen Poe

CHAPTER 17

## CHEMICAL REACTION

I awoke early, before the sun. At 10 AM I had my first appointment in the chemo lab. In preparation, I stood in the shower for a long time and let the steaming water rain down on me. At last I turned off the water, wrapped myself in a towel and reclined in a mossy-green lounge chair in my library.

Through the magic of ear buds, Dr. Bernie Segal mentally prepared me for the impending experience — my first chemo treatment — my first weed-n-feed. I vigorously rubbed my worry stone between my thumb and index finger as I listened to his soothing words.

I must have fallen asleep because Hermes and Flit stood at the side of my chair. They had completed concocting the magical serum. The time had come. My body shook violently. I opened my eyes. I was once more in my home. My husband stood over me. "We have to go," he explained apologetically.

I ran upstairs, threw on some clothes and popped an anti-nausea pill. We drove to the lab in silence.

Once at the lab a young woman, who had walked this path before me, started an IV and began administering pre-meds. The weed killer would follow.

The medicine dripped slowly into my veins. My eyesight blurred. My head roared as though a freight train ran the distance between my ears. Shadows came to life and danced on the walls next to me. I closed my eyes.

The next time I opened them I was back in Flit's little cottage. I could see her smile down on me. She sat on my chest as everything spun faster and faster. She laid the back of her tiny hand on my forehead and patted my cheek. I squeezed my eyes tightly shut. When I opened them I was back in the chemo lab. I called the nurse over.

Wide-eyed and scared, "I'm seeing things," I told her.

"It's just the Benadryl Buzz. Try to sleep. You'll be fine," the nurse assured me.

I dozed off and found myself back at Flit's. She covered me up with a patchwork quilt artfully assembled from fabric ripped and torn from my past. She gently kissed my cheek. "You're doing great!" she told me as she shuffled off to feed her raccoons.

The earth dropped away from beneath me. I fell backwards through space and time. I awoke in a hospital room clinging to the still warm hand of a dying Snowman from winters past. It was early afternoon and bitterly cold. The sun flooded through the window, brilliant and icy.

Bracing myself, I sat up and asked, "Is it more important to inhale or to exhale?" I suddenly needed to know the answer to that question more than anything else in the world.

"Exhale," the Snowman breathlessly replied.

"I thought so," I squeezed his hand and we both closed our eyes. He's right, I thought. The energy comes from the release.

A voice cut through the mist. "You're all done for today." It was the nurse.

With the first treatment behind me, I exhaled long and slow. It was over. Four hours had passed in the blink-of-an-eye. I staggered to the car, and went home to sleep it off.

In the morning as I washed my face, I studied my reflection in the mirror. I recognized myself. Still I looked weird, different, some of my features belonged to... a turtle.

"Patience, my Dear, and perseverance," said the turtle reflected in the mirror. I dropped the soap and threw up in the toilet.

Every two weeks the magic elixir entered my veins. Every two weeks I resembled the turtle more.

Seventeen days after my first chemo treatment — and three days after my most recent infusion, I clamored from my bed leaving half my hair on the pillow. I crouched on my hands and knees on the floor next to my bed, my head whirling.

My hair, including the ones inside my nose, could no longer hang on and neither could I. I wanted to eat junk food. I wanted to stow away on the Orient Express. I wanted to become two-dimensional, black and white, and float around in a flowing satin negligee with matching peignoir like Lauren Bacall. I wanted to jump from my window and fly to Neverland with Peter Pan and Wendy. More than anything else I wanted to quit. The nagging one-hundred-thousand-dollar question was how badly did I want to live?

When I finished chemo I would still have to face another surgery, thirty-six treatments of radiation and five years of pills. *If I let them put me under anesthesia again, what if I never wake up?* I became paralyzed with fear. I needed strength. I needed a push.

"Exhale!" I heard the Snowman's words once more.

*Let it go,* I reminded myself.

It had been thirteen years since that conversation with the Snowman, but the memory gave me comfort. I was not alone. His life, his memories and his words strengthened me and helped me to go on.

I pushed fear, hopelessness, and resentment out of the way. I had to make room for what wanted to come in.

I had things to do. First and foremost, I had to find eyebrows. *If I had eyebrows I wouldn't look **too** bad,* I flattered myself. I did extensive facial-hair-for-the-facial-hairless research and headed for Sephora. I bought the Anastasia eyebrow kit with stencils. it came with five varying arches from petite to full, a powder and brush – to fill in the space where once hair grew (I chose the medium ash color), and a gel to hold it all in place.

With a stylish scarf and artfully painted on brows, I continued on. After all, I had places I still wanted to visit and a boy who was counting on me to raise him. I exhaled deeply.

## CHAPTER 18

# FRED IS DEAD

I heard through the chemo pick-line that Fred was dead. Fred and I were strangers who shared a disease. From my distant perspective, I could read the writing on the billboard of his soul. We met in an oncology waiting room in Wisconsin on a cold and gloomy October morning. He loved the desert – Arizona to be exact. He advertised that love through his clothing. If Fred were a plant, he would be a cholla – a teddy bear cholla. I'd venture to guess that Fred's entire internal garden landscape resembled the Sonoran desert.

Autumn turned to winter. As the days shortened, the cold, damp air and lack of sunbeams withered Fred's spines and zapped his sap.

The last time we met, I could see in his eyes that he was resigned to die. Perhaps he couldn't face the winter. Perhaps he was just cold and faded. An invisible thread binds all who share a disease. When one gives up the fight, the rest of us stare horrified at our own mortality. I urged him to fight. He couldn't. Or he wouldn't.

"Please, Fred. Make the doctor give you what you need to live," I pleaded.

Fred just smiled, pulled his ASU ball cap down over his eyes and rested his head back on the pastel, tweed sofa cushions. He looked peaceful, tired, and old. Our conversation was closed. Perhaps no doctor could prescribe what Fred needed. I would never know. That's the last time we saw each other.

I think each of us has a secret language that he or she thinks is so unbelievably simple that anyone who cares for us would be able to decipher it. But, that's a lie. Perspective is everything. What is simple for one to see can be invisible to another. I'm not taking any chances. I will not leave this world assuming that my family and friends don't care for me just because they can't decipher my secret code. I will ask. Out loud. In words. It may be scary. I may feel selfish, but I will ask. I do not wish on my family the regrets of realizing, in five years, that perhaps I had a reason to live. A reason I never voiced, but thought they all knew.

I was pulled back from my memories of Fred by the sound of my name. A recliner in the chemo lab had opened up. I had been summoned, once again, for my Taxol treatment. As the premeds hit my bloodstream, nausea and anti-nausea, histamines and Benadryl, Fred's death and my life pushed and pulled for control. I began to spin and buzz.

As the waves of nausea ebbed and flowed within me, I could see myself walking in violent surf. Fred's lifeless body bobbed face-down in the waves next to me. I became racked with fear and guilt – fear for my life and guilt that I was alive and Fred wasn't.

Fred's corpse tried to drag me underwater and suffocate me.

I fought off the urge to call the nurse as silent tears streamed down my face. I closed my eyes and tried to relax. Panic throbbed against my throat and in my chest. The rhythm clashed against the accelerating cadence of my heart.

*Exhale,* I reminded myself. Just four hours today then I've only got two more treatments. I can do this.

*No I can't. I have to call the nurse and get out of here,* another voice inside me protested.

The waves knocked me down, and the riptide tried to pull me out to sea, but I refused to go. I pushed myself up and continued to walk. As the surf rushed forward, Fred's body slammed against my legs. The waves relentlessly knocked me down again and again. Each time I stood once more. Each time I took a step forward. The surge forced me to my knees. The riptide called me back to the sea. *I'm tired. I just want to rest,* I thought.

I didn't stand. I sank below the surface. The firm sand at the bottom comforted me. My body quivered. I opened my eyes. *Where am I?* I took a moment to survey my surroundings. A face came into focus. I was elated to see Gloria, my nurse!

She gently rocked my shoulders. "You're all done for today," she said as she smiled warmly. "Are you okay?"

I nodded although not entirely sure I was. My eyes darted around the room. Fred's lifeless body had vanished. I lay once again in a recliner in a chemo lab; *The Wild Wild West* played loudly on the TV above me. My clothes, my legs, my feet were all dry. Only my face dripped wet and salty. Was it spray from the surf, or the cold, clammy condensation of fear and sickness? I steadied my legs and stood once more. I navigated my way, through the waves of nausea, to the car. I went home. I threw up. I slept. *Only two treatments to go,* I reassured myself and exhaled once more as I struggled with the ever-present urge to quit.

*Courage doesn't always roar. Sometimes courage*
*is the quiet voice at the end of the day saying,*
*"I will try again tomorrow."*

————— Mary Anne Radmacher

CHAPTER 19

# QUIET GUY

Two weeks later, I entered the lab for my seventh, and next-to-last, treatment.

Haley and Hannah chatted pleasantly about cooking. On the TV near the ceiling an overweight man with stringy, blond hair and a white apron poured marinade over a rump roast. Only one free recliner remained and it was next to Quiet Guy. *I hate sitting next to Quiet Guy,* I told myself. *He's so quiet I don't even know his name.* Reluctantly, I took my seat and a nurse started an IV. A former patient came around and gave us all bananas.

As the medicine hit my bloodstream my heart-rate steadily climbed. The beating in my ear drums intensified and gathered momentum. I was getting good at monitoring my own heart rate. It plateaued at just under 115 beats per minute. I assured myself there was no reason to call the nurse. I closed my eyes and tried to relax. *Exhale,* I reminded myself for the hundredth time. *Only four more hours. After this, only one more treatment. Don't quit now.* If I pushed the button, I'd have to start again. *Would I? I don't remember. I can do this.*

*No, I can't! I can't do it! I have to call the nurse,* a second, panic-stricken voice inside me screamed.

Quiet guy next to me turned ashen and beat me to the call button. He was having trouble breathing. He looked bad. This was his third treatment and his third allergic reaction.

The doctor and four nurses rushed in. Doc, usually calm and convincing, appeared visibly shaken. *Oh, this is bad, very bad.* I no longer felt my own racing heart. Instead, my heart went out to Quiet Guy.

Doc quickly pushed a syringe of clear liquid into Quiet Guy's IV. As we all waited for the anti-reaction meds to take effect, Doc explained to himself, as much as to the rest of us, that usually by the second treatment, the body adjusted. That bit of trivia didn't seem to soothe Quiet Guy.

Time stood still. Regardless of the odds, Death marched steadily toward Quiet Guy's door and we all knew it. His chest looked as though it might explode before the medication had a chance to work. He arched his back. *Is he in pain? Is his heart going to stop flipping-out or stop beating altogether?* I wondered as I waited.

Finally the anti-reaction medication worked and the color began to seep back into Quiet Guy's face. Doc assured him that in a matter of moments he would begin to feel better. He no longer arched his back. His chest relaxed. He would live another day, but his treatment and his capacity to fight were finished.

Perhaps an hour had passed since I arrived in the lab. In that short span of time, Quiet Guy raised the white flag. He refused to battle. He and his will wasted away.

Quiet Guy quietly left the room. The rest of us reclined in silence. No one felt much like talking about marinades and rump roasts anymore.

*What saves a man is to take a step.*
*Then another step.  It is always the same step,*
*but you have to take it.*

Wind, Sand and Stars ———— Antoine de Saint-Exupéry

*Just as it is known*
*That an image of one's face is seen*
*Depending on a mirror*
*But does not really exist as a face,*
*So the conception of "I" exists*
*Dependent on mind and body,*
*But like the image of a face*
*The "I" does not at all exist as its own reality.*

Precious Garland of Advice ————— Nagarjuna's

CHAPTER 20

# TURTLE REFLECTS

I had chemo completely behind me. That was the good news. The bad news? The turtle I met reflected in the mirror after my first treatment had nearly taken over.

My skin creased and hardened into a leathery composition. Not a single hair remained on my face, my body, my head. Even my eyelids became red, puffy and lash free. My neck contracted. A hump formed between my shoulder blades. My body rounded.

During the weeks of chemo most days I felt sick to my stomach. If I got hungry, I heaved. When I ate I felt less sick. So I ate — often. I kept crackers on the night stand by my bed. Even in the middle of the night, I ate. Although on high doses of chemo every two weeks, although I thought cancer and chemo patients became emaciated, I faithfully gained one to two pounds per week — every week. I got fat. Fat was better than sick. Then I got fatter.

I felt safe in my newfound cushion of fat. It protected me — isolated me. Fat became my barrier from reality. I hid behind my shield of fat and I ate until not a single stitch of clothes I owned fit. Undeterred, I bought new clothes and ate some more.

The last bastion of my pretty packaging was gone. I stared in the mirror. I moved in closer. I had no hair, no eyebrows and no eyelashes. My waistline had widened and my body formed an oval. I tipped my head sideways and cupped my hands around my right eye to shade the glare. I looked hard, trying to find myself. Was I still in there? An old, sallow turtle gawked blankly back at me. We both blinked.

All my life I cared what other people thought. I cared if they liked me or not. I cared if I was pretty. In sixteen long weeks all vestiges of beauty had gone, but with them the importance of external beauty had also gone. It became less and less important to me. I became more acquainted with the turtle and I liked her. Maybe she wasn't so bad after all. At the end of week eight instead of throwing up at the sight of her I smiled and welcomed her warmly. Unlike mine, her beauty sprang from within.

Instead of spending my time worry about beauty and what other people thought of me, I dove down below the surface and tended my garden. I became calmer, less judgmental of others as well as myself. I realized that my life affected others in only superficial ways. My life was mine to do something wonderful or something mediocre with. Perhaps each man is an island — or at least tends an island garden.

Week after week more weeds withered, shriveled and died. Soon I would raze what remained to smoldering ashes. *Perhaps I have a chance after all,* I silently hoped.

CHAPTER 21

# BLEED AND BLOSSOM

One particularly difficult change arrived with the removal of my ovaries. Pathologically speaking, my cancer was strongly receptive to estrogen and progesterone. The less of these hormones I had, the less hospitable my body would be for cancer to grow.

We needed to cut her supply chain. As soon as I finished with chemo, two surgeons met me at the hospital. One came to remove the rest of the cancer; the other came to take my ovaries. I would awaken postmenopausal.

I was slow to embrace the child-bearing years, now that they were chemically, surgically and irrevocably gone. I missed them. More than I thought I would, I missed them.

Gentlemen, I'm about to embark on a journey that concerns the ladies — particularly the young ladies. Let this serve as a warning to you men who can't handle the truth. Skip ahead to the next chapter immediately 'cuz we're diving head first into the subject of the monthly bleed ——————— now.

The rose – a long time symbol for the blooming of femininity —
has thorns. When the rose strikes, we blossom and we bleed. It's a
packaged deal.

Many men throughout history have not been particularly
empathetic about the woes of the rose. We women too often refer
to menstruation as the monthly curse. In truth womanhood and the
ability to have children comes in a nifty, little, red package exquisitely
balanced.

One summer of discovery, back in my late twenties, a friend
invited me to take part in a Native-American sweat-lodge ceremony.
The ceremony took place in the backyard of a suburban dwelling in an
upper-middle-class neighborhood north of San Francisco. Although
the yard had a privacy fence around it, all the surrounding homes were
two stories. Still we pale, culturally and mystically devoid white women
— in our quest for a magical, mystical, meaning-of-life moment —
pranced around the backyard in nothing more than our birthday suits
and a beach towel. We were lost at sea and searching for a direction to
which we could set our psychic compasses. A suburban sweat-lodge
seemed like the perfect remedy for our communal, spiritual malaise.

A Sioux warrior and his grandmother flew in from South Dakota
to bestow authenticity to our vision quest. Sioux Grandmother took
us into the lodge. We sat Indian-style in a circle until the organizer of
the occasion informed us that it was unladylike for us to sit with our
"pussies wide open." We rearranged our appendages so that our feet
rested together on the left while our knees remained touching on the
right. As Grandmother poured cool water over hot rocks, the air sizzled
and stung my nostrils. I inhaled slowly, methodically. Many women
panicked and begged to be let out. ı welcomed the closeness of the air.
It sheltered me. The darkness and heat hugged me, and I felt at home.

After our time of sweat, heat and purification we all sat in a semi-
circle honoring the Sioux warrior and his grandmother. We thanked
them both for making the long journey to California. We then eagerly

awaited ancient wisdom and enchanted storytelling.

After a long pause, the warrior opened his mouth. As his slow, methodical voice lilted through the air a faint smell of beer and cigarettes wafted past me. "We Sioux can smell the moon!" his voice boomed.

I was wowed! I'd never smelled the moon. I leaned forward as I eagerly awaited with bated breath a chance to learn how to smell the moon.

"All women must know that her moon is disgusting," he continued. "Every Sioux woman has the good sense to leave the tribe while on her moon. She knows her vile stench pollutes the air."

*What the hell is he talking about?* I wondered.

He paused. We all looked around at each other and shrugged.

"There is one among you who is on her moon. The awful pong burns my nostrils. She must leave." He pointed emphatically toward the garden gate. His eyes scanned the stunned crowd — resting just long enough on each woman to make her shrink in self-loathing at being feminine. For an uncomfortably long time nobody spoke and nobody moved.

I awkwardly got up and went into the bathroom just to check. I thought maybe he scared me into bleeding even though it was nowhere near my time to cycle. *Nope. Nothing.* I came back out and looked him right in the eye. I shook my head and, with a click and a wink, I gave him the all-clear thumbs-up and took my seat.

We all waited patiently but nobody claimed her moon. The Sioux warrior refused to have anything more to do with us and abruptly left. For a moment I felt ashamed to be a woman. I felt dirty. Then I felt desecrated and violated.

Other than my encounter with the Sioux warrior, I never felt dirty or ashamed at being a woman. I didn't particularly like menstruating, who does? For the most part, I didn't even like men viewing me as a sexual goddess. Now that my ovaries were gone; however, I missed them. I missed them physically and emotionally. Severe headaches and uncontrollable upwelling of emotions became the norm. Gone forever was the possibility of having another child. Gone, hopefully not forever, was my waistline.

CHAPTER 22

# THE CHICKEN OR THE EGG

I felt old. I realized I was no longer a spring chicken.

"Hermes, if you're not busy, I need you." I called out into the darkness. I used to beseech any and all gods within the sound of my voice. Since Hermes had answered my call, this time I took the liberty of requesting him personally. He didn't seem to mind.

"What is it? What's so urgent?" He asked.

"Which came first the chicken or the egg?"

Hermes studied my face for a long time as if to determine whether or not I was serious and whether or not I could handle the truth. After much contemplation, "the egg," he answered unceremoniously.

"What do you mean the egg? I always thought it was the chicken. How do you get an egg without a chicken?"

Hermes sighed. "I can see this is going to take a while. Let's walk," he replied. As we began to walk along the banks of a slow-moving stream, he added, "The world is full of eggs without chickens."

I wanted answers — answers about chickens and eggs, cause and effect. I wanted order. I wanted life to make sense.

In the past, I read many books that claimed we each have the power to create our own universe completely, through our thoughts

— through our intentions. "Is each negative event created by a negative thought?" I asked Hermes.

"Some things just are. If you spend too much time and energy wishing things were different, you will miss the beauty in what is. The mayfly does not wish for long life. The turtle does not wish for speed. What is, is." Hermes placed a hand tenderly on my shoulder.

We walked along as his words quietly scrubbed some of the residual stuck-on guilt from my corners. Silent tears washed the loosened gunk down the drain and flushed it away. I felt refreshed, if not squeaky clean.

Perhaps I would never know completely which comes first, a thought or an event. Maybe events and thoughts interact more like addition and multiplication equations and less like subtraction or division or connect-the-dots. Maybe the order of things really isn't that important to the outcome. *If not, then what is?* I think I'll shelve that thought for later. Right now Hermes and I have bigger eggs to fry.

Hermes motioned toward a large cottonwood tree near the banks of the stream. "Sit down."

I smiled to myself, warmed by his choice of location and happy to finally find out once and for all which came first, the chicken or the egg. We sat down in the shade of the long-standing tree, and he began to explain. He spoke in a manner usually reserved for toddlers. As he did, he pulled the words from his throat with his hands. He opened his eyes wide and nodded his head. "Everything," he began tentatively, "I mean every thought, every person, every time, every place, every idea, every animal, vegetable and mineral, every planet, star, black hole, every concept, every question and every answer —— You get the idea? Everything." His words chugged from his lips like a cumbersome freight train leaving the station. "Everything was once contained in a single egg."

His words pulled me forward onto the newly constructed tracks. "Whoa, that had to be some egg." I leaned back and applied the brakes.

Hermes smiled and shook his head. "Instead of a chicken egg, try to imagine it more like a... a... well, a frog egg or a fish egg, but denser. Much, much, denser. So dense, in fact, that this egg could fit in the palm of my hand. And this egg continued to contract. It became smaller and denser, smaller and denser, smaller and denser. Then one day the moment of birth arrived, and the egg began to hatch." He shrugged and wrinkled up one side of his face as if to say, "That's it."

*What a load of crap,* I thought. I shook my head and snorted like a bull. Fifty million questions raced around me. I looked left, then right trying to grasp any question — a starting point. "Well, what was inside this... egg?" I ultimately asked.

"Weren't you listening? Everything! Well ——— and nothing." Hermes closed his eyes and took a deep breath. He placed his head in his hands. For a long time he didn't speak. Then he looked up at me and smiled. "Soup. It contained soup. Not chunky soup, more like a really thick broth — a thick broth in which each droplet was identical to every other droplet."

"Soup? Is that the best you got?"

"Yes. Soup."

"Well how in the world does a soup egg hatch?"

Hermes laughed out loud. "Slowly. Very slowly." He chuckled again. "In fact, it's still hatching." He good-naturedly patted me on the back. "Come on. Let's get some lunch. How about macaroni and cheese?"

*WHENE'ER companions don't agree,*
*They work without accord;*
*And naught but trouble doth result,*
*Although they all work hard.*

*One day a swan, a pike, a crab,*
*Resolved a load to haul;*
*All three were harnessed to the cart,*
*And pulled together all.*
*But though they pulled with all their might,*
*The cart-load on the bank stuck tight.*
*The swan pulled upward to the skies;*
*The crab did backward crawl;*
*The pike made for the water straight —*
*It proved no use at all!*

*Now, which of them was most to blame*
*'Tis not for me to say;*
*But this I know: the load is there*
*Unto this very day.*

———— Ivan Krylov

CHAPTER 23

# MACARONI AND CHEESE

Until now, I had no idea that Greek gods even ate macaroni and cheese. Hermes made a delicious batch from scratch.

I was hungry, so I took a bite. It tasted delicious. As I rolled the elbow noodles and velvety sauce around in my mouth, I wondered how many steps it took to make the kind of macaroni and cheese that I made — the stuff from a box.

I mentally walked myself through the process. First, boil the noodles; then, drain them; add the cheese powder; some milk and some butter; stir and enjoy. Let's see, that would be six, maybe seven steps.

I recalled making a family-sized box just last month. I stood in my kitchen whipping up a batch of this miraculous glob of unnaturally-orange goodness. While I efficiently approached the noodle-boiling phase, my mom entered the kitchen and unceremoniously informed me that I was doing it **all wrong**.

This is a box of macaroni and cheese we're talking about, people! I struggled financially through college. For five years I lived on the stuff. I thought myself somewhat of an expert on the subject only to discover, now, that I'd been making it all wrong for over twenty years.

As she explained the proper amount of water needed for optimal-noodle-boilage, she gently placed her left hand on my shoulder. "It's okay, honey; we can't all be expert macaroni and cheese makers. Allow me to do this for you," she said with her eyes although with her mouth she hadn't uttered a word. She extended her right hand, palm up, and motioned, almost imperceptibly with her head and with her eyebrows toward a wooden spoon I was holding. Her body language urged, "Relinquish control of the spoon, Kristine."

We faced off for quite some time. She liked to cook for me. Every other time she entered my kitchen I gave up the spoon. It made her happy. This time however something weird came over me. This time I clung to the spoon like a life raft. I chose my words carefully and spoke slowly — my voice full of concern.

"Mom," I began, "it's macaroni and cheese — out of a box. I can do this. Believe it or not, I've been doing it for over twenty years now. Trust me. It will be okay. You'll see. It may not be nearly as tasty as yours, but it will be edible. Please, go sit down. Dinner will be ready in ten minutes."

Dejectedly she left the kitchen.

I finished cooking. We ate. Then a funny thing happened. Her eyes filled with sadness and with pride. She complimented me on the meal. Perhaps for the first time, she saw me not only as her child, but as a wife, a competent mother and a woman in my own right. Whatever happened, our relationship was never the same. (It's better.)

Why am I telling you all of this? Simple. I believe that if I bought fifty boxes of macaroni and cheese; and I asked fifty different people to make it; we'd have quite a variety of ways to process through the steps.

Some potential chefs would use a big pan. Others would choose to go small. A few may even use a fry pan. Maybe it's the only pan they have. I would use two quarts of water while my mom would opt for more in the neighborhood of six gallons. Several people may melt the butter in with the noodles then add the milk and then add the powdered cheese. Others may pre-melt the butter in the microwave (dare I say it?) with the milk.

The steps are all the same. The way each of us processes through the steps is as varied as we are. And the end result? It's all macaroni and cheese, and it's all delicious.

That's life!

On life's journey, it's often been hard for me to pick my own path. I'm riddled with self-doubt. And there's no shortage of people willing to tell me that my path is wrong or that I should take another way. Where I come from we say, "There's more than one way to skin a cat." How horrifying is that?! I like the sentiment, but never cared for the imagery. Now, instead of envisioning a skinned cat, I just picture macaroni and cheese. It gets the same point across, and it's a lot easier to swallow.

We're all born. If we live long enough, we'll all go through the same steps, the same phases of life. We'll each get through these steps a little (or a lot) differently. In the end, we'll all die. If my way is right does, that make yours wrong? No. Is my way better than yours? No. Some ways may seem faster or more efficient, but this is not a race. As long as all the steps are completed, there's no right or wrong way to travel through life. Just keep going. Skin that cat. Make that box of macaroni and cheese and enjoy.

*It is our less conscious thoughts*
*and our less conscious actions*
*which mainly mold our lives*
*and the lives of those*
*who spring from us.*

——————— Samuel Butler

CHAPTER 24

# THE SONG

Although I was completely unaware, quite often, someone or something inside of me sang a song of past failures and present flaws. The song, bypassing my ears, reached down deeply, twisting my guts. It lulled me toward despair. As my body reacted chemically and organically I began to feel like crap.

Finally, from the darkness, another voice, small and soothing said, "Find someone to help you hear the song, then begin again." This voice emanated from my stomach, just below the navel. Feeling depressed, I closed my eyes and tried to sleep.

I awoke to a thum-thrum-drumming on my forehead. I opened my eyes to find myself face to face with a persistent, cross-dressing somewhat overweight caterpillar in a colorful salsa gown.

"Ah, good, you're up!" he proclaimed as he continued to hammer out a calypso beat on my face.

"Please Mr. Caterpillar, stop. I have an awful headache," I pleaded. I rolled onto my side and curled up in a ball, shielding my head with my arms.

"I see." He stopped drumming and did a couple of turns and

shimmies before removing a large basket of fruit from the top of his head. He deftly set it on the ground beside him.

"Can you help me, Mr. Caterpillar? I mean, I need to hear a song. Not just any song, **the** song. The song that plays in my head and in my body. The song that pulls me down. The song that makes me sad."

"Oh, I see. That song." The caterpillar nodded in understanding. "You can't hear that song with your ears. You must listen instead with your spleen and with your tonsils." He tugged thoughtfully at the colorful ruffles of his bolero. "They will warn you of the song," he stated in over-annunciated consonants and rotund vowels.

"I don't understand."

"First you must find the cord — what I mean to say is, find what you want to let go of and grasp it — like you would a crawdad." The caterpillar threw me a toothy grin.

"Why do I want to grasp what I want to let go of? That doesn't make any sense," I said.

The caterpillar covered half his mouth with a chubby foot, one from the back half of his body. "Pssst." He pointed that foot quickly in my direction. "Shut-up and listen," he grumbled before forming a "V" with his body and throwing all his legs in the air.

"You ready?" He turned his face to me and opened his eyes wide.

I knew better than to interrupt again.

"Then let's begin." He rolled over onto his stomach and propped his front half up onto his elbows. "We'll start with *sad*. Connected to *sad* you'll find a tiny cord of emotion. Actually, it could be connected to misery or woe or fretful angst, it doesn't really matter — pick one. Catch it. Then follow the cord. That is where and how you begin."

He pulled and tugged at his face until it resembled a giant nose. He sniffed at the air. "There," he pointed emphatically off in the distance with four of his legs, "or it could be over there." He pointed in the opposite direction. "Actually, I have no idea, and it doesn't really matter. Only you can hunt it down. Find it. Observe it. Expand it. Because once you detect it, you can yank out the power cord," he assured me.

"You're not making any sense. And anyway, I had my tonsils out when I was five years old."

"Keep up!" he scolded.

Sometimes it's just a picture," he continued as he made a square in the air with his legs. "Don't try so hard, just follow the cord back to the thought you had right before you began to feel like, sad or like, angry, you know?" "Then look inside your head." He knocked on his own head. (It made a hollow, wooden sound), "Look at the picture. What does it mean to you?"

"I must be a moron because I have no idea what you're talking about!" I screamed in frustration.

"I must be a moron," the caterpillar repeated, shrugging his shoulders and bouncing slightly up and down. He mimicked my voice perfectly.

"Now, we're getting somewhere." The caterpillar rubbed his palms together and licked his lips. "Excellent!"

"Where?" I asked.

"Why, to the beginning!" The caterpillar proclaimed in exaltation. He raised his hands to the sky. Then he bent down and grasped the basket of fruit from the ground and placed it back atop his head. He stood up. "I think better when I dance," he said as he began to rumba. "Just work with me here. State to yourself, deliberately and out-loud, the direct opposite of what you just said."

"You mean the opposite of 'I must be a moron'? I'm," I wiggled my fingers in front of my face, "I don't know," I snorted. "I'm... Albert Einstein."

"Good! Say it again and this time, see it and be it, baby." The caterpillar gave me a shimmy and a wink.

"I'm Albert Einstein." I pictured myself in black and white with wild, salt-and-pepper hair, a mustache and sockless feet in men's dress shoes. "That's ridiculous!" I laughed.

The caterpillar's eyes grew very large; receding, wispy white hair covered his green head. He pulled at his tiny ears until they became long and pointy. He looked like Yoda. "Ridiculous, you say," he began in a wise and raspy voice. "One extreme cannot be ridiculous without its opposite being equally as ridiculous, young padawan. This exercise in balance moves you out of extremes and back into stability." The caterpillar placed his palms together as if to pray and bowed deeply.

*He does a pretty good Yoda impression,* I thought, *but Yoda wouldn't be caught dead in that dress.* I chuckled. I wondered if I'd laughed out loud. *I shouldn't do that,* I told myself. *He's very nice, and he's helping me. I hope I didn't offend him.* My mood and my face dropped. I felt as though I were a terrible person for laughing at the caterpillar the way I did.

"Who makes these rules?" he asked.

"What do you mean?" I tried to pretend I had no idea what he was talking about.

"I shouldn't do that," the caterpillar replied. He read my thoughts and, once again, mimicked my voice perfectly. "Who says?" He continued to question me.

"I'm tired. I want to quit for today," I sighed.

"Are you sure you should?" He cajoled. "Should, shouldn't, ought to, must, can't..." The caterpillar's voice trailed off. He was gone.

I leaned forward to see if he had really gone. I sighed and relaxed. My stomach puffed out over the top of my jeans. Wow, they're getting tight. Ugh, am I fat! And ugly. And bald. I can't go out in public like this. I should never have allowed myself to get so fat. I'm weak.

The words continued to beat me down. At first I felt horrible and then I smiled. It wasn't me talking, it was that song again. For the first time I heard it and recognized it for what it was.

"I hear you," I whispered as I grasped hold of the cord, "and I am so beautiful and thin, oh, and tall that I'm often mistaken for a super model." I laughed out loud as I pictured myself on a runway in Paris.

Like the caterpillar taught me, I yanked the cord from its power source and the two images in my mind canceled each other out. "I'm cured!" I yelled out loud.

But I wasn't. Hearing the song was only one step on a very long journey. It was a good step — a positive step, a step in the right direction, but just one baby step of many more to follow.

Inside of each of us lives a little person who doesn't like change. This little man enjoys being small. As I pushed the boundaries of my life, the song became more persistent. I eventually understood that the goal of the song was to keep me from expanding my horizons. The more I stretched my world, the more often I heard the song. I soon welcomed the song as an indicator of growth.

I no longer cursed the mistakes I made. I let them go and looked upward to the future. I reassured myself by enjoying where I now stood. I no longer berated myself for past mistakes. I no longer analyzed the validity of the steps along the way. These steps, right or wrong, had brought me to this point — a point I needed to reach — a point of change.

Before reaching this point, I had become so domesticated that my instincts had all but vanished. With no code of conduct, without the should and should nots in life, I acted on impulse. If I felt tired, I slept. If I felt hungry, I ate. If I felt happy, I laughed. The guilt that surrounded these seemingly simple tasks was gone.

That first night I slept from 7 PM until 2 AM. I awoke and did three hours of thinking, writing, meditating and yoga. I then slept peacefully until my husband began to stir beside me. Through the darkness I whispered, "Morning came twice today. I love mornings." It was fall — well after Labor Day. *Today, I'll wear white,* I thought. I donned my most sparkling white, men's, V-neck, Fruit-of-the-Loom T-shirt — without a bra.

Filled with hope and anticipation, I greeted the new day.

*I dream my painting and then paint my dream.*

——— Vincent Van Gogh

CHAPTER 25

# JIGSAW PUZZLE

I like piles. Everything's handy and accessible in piles. Piles work better for me than a filing cabinet. I tended to hang onto everything — for sentimentality or control. This has led to some mighty big piles. I had piles of events, piles of beliefs, piles of reactions. I'd also accumulated piles of interactions, piles of emotions. I could go on and on. As I mentioned before, I like piles.

When I was diagnosed with cancer I began sifting through the clutter searching for answers. None came. I frantically rifled through my piles. I flung the color-coded contents skyward. When the dust settled the canvas of my life resembled a Jackson Pollack painting. I couldn't glean any larger meaning from the hit-and-miss splatters of color.

Unhappy and disenfranchised, I remembered a quote from Vincent Van Gogh. "I dream my painting and then paint my dream." Instead of making more piles or haphazardly flinging the events of my life skyward, I decided to use the events that colored my life like pieces of a jigsaw puzzle.

I formulated a goal. I considered what I wanted the resulting representation of my life to look like. I burned this image onto my mind. I began to shape my destiny — my impact on the world, with the raw materials given me. I knew it was important to me that the seemingly random events of my life related to one another in ways that made the whole picture more powerful than the sum of its pieces.

I gazed back at my piles. For the first time, I was actually excited and happy to have so much baggage; it gave me more color and more puzzle pieces to work with. I began to methodically join the pieces together. Most pieces held beauty or meaning and value. The pieces that didn't were still vital to the puzzle.

When I felt particularly pissed-off or I found myself wallowing in self-pity over a single puzzle piece I studied the emerging portrayal of my life. I realized that my painting, my impact, would not be the same without that piece. This connection to the whole makes any given puzzle piece worth the cost. After all, without it, the entire impression could not possibly be the same. This goes for all of the pieces — yes, even the black ones.

Maybe that's the only true meaning of life — to take what we are given, make something beautiful out of it and give it back before we go.

Each moment, each event fits perfectly in the place created for it. You can understand each piece entirely. What shape it is. What colors it is. What size it is. But, the true story — the true representation of that piece is not fully known until you understand the relationship it has to all the other pieces of the puzzle. Facts cannot help you understand this relationship. Trial and error and truth can. Only through attempting to fit the pieces together, can the roles they play in the bigger picture begin to be understood.

We are not defined by the images on the individual puzzle pieces — a mom, a social worker, a Methodist — or by physical attributes — a brunette, a tall-drink-of-water, or the girl next door. We are the works of art created from those pieces.

The puzzle pieces you accumulate and how you use them will

ultimately make up the canvas of your life. Events just are. We breathe life and meaning into them. How we relate to the events of our lives matters. We each choose for ourselves the significance of those events and how we place them into our emerging portraits.

*To go beyond is as wrong as to fall short*

——— Confucius

CHAPTER 26

# THE ZENITH

I f we live long enough we all reach that space between accumulating and downsizing, between physical and spiritual, between micro and macro — in other words that moment when we comprehend that from here on out, life is all downhill. I still shudder when I recall the weightlessness I felt when I first recognized that I had indeed reached the zenith of my life. Not wanting to admit that I was over-the-hill, I had in fact over-climbed. I subsequently spun out of control and began to free fall.

I slammed face first onto the peak of existence before sliding down a slippery slope toward a sheer drop-off. As I skidded backward every single, silky strand of Miss-Clairol-Perfect-Ten-Ready-Made-Cupcake-neutral-medium-blonde hair fell out of my head. The once brassy and sassy blonde now resembled a puffy, partially eaten, partially dehydrated apple with a Brillo pad resting atop her head. No matter how much product I used, my hair retained a lavender hue and that tight, fresh-from-the-beauty-shop-wash-and-set charm. I could no longer reach the buckles of my bra. I had to clasp the hooks in the front, spin the bra 180 degrees, then struggle to insert my shoulders into the straps.

After the battle of the bra, I'd have to sit down and catch my breath.

Although I'd reached mid-life on the fast track, eventually I stopped falling. It was then I understood that life, as I knew it, was over. Soon I would slip slowly away or worse yet, I'd become my mother. Not that I don't love and respect my mother, I do. I just didn't want to **be** her.

We live in an age of youth and skin-deep beauty. Mid-life signifies the nail in the coffin. I bravely faced the miracle of the middle head on. For an instant I neither waxed nor waned. A bittersweet tranquility inhabited this vacuum between becoming and withdrawing. Tomorrow I may wither and fade, but for that single moment, I burst forth with life, and I realized, *I'm not dead, I'm just old!*

I diligently carved my life into paper thin slices and placed each sliver between two panes of glass. I examined each slice carefully under the brightly-lit magnification of a microscope. I'd spent my life accumulating things, abilities, knowledge. I didn't really have the time to use any of this stuff. I was too busy gaining it — acquiring more and more and more.

We all do, until we don't. Then we experience the primordial impulse to share our accumulated uniqueness with the world. If you've accumulated wealth, you may wish to spend money freely on frivolous toys and fast cars. If you've accumulated an amazing talent in the art of the mambo, horizontal or otherwise, you may experience a sudden itch to share that talent with as many dancers as possible. The urge is primal, instinctive.

I'm convinced that if we honor the longing to give back — if we admit to ourselves that we've turned the corner and are in fact over-the-hill, we can share our lives in ways that are less destructive to ourselves and to our families. Let's face it, downhill is easier ground to cover. Each one of us, in some unique way, can help those who still struggle to climb that mountain. The second half of life is our chance to give back — to groom the trails for those who come after us.

*The most important words in mid-life are – Let Go. Let it happen to you. Let it happen to your partner. Let the feelings, Let the changes … You are moving out of roles and into the self … it would be surprising if we didn't experience some pain as we leave the familiarity of one adult stage for the uncertainty of the next. But the willingness to move through each passage is equivalent to the willingness to live abundantly. If we don't change, we don't grow. If we don't grow, we are not really living.*

———— Gail Sheehy

*Who may regret what was,*
*since it has made Himself himself?*
*All that I was I am,*
*And the old childish joy now lives in me*
*At sight of a green field or a green tree.*

*All That I was I Am* ———————— John Freeman

CHAPTER 27

# WHO ARE YOU?

I heard his voice in the void. I couldn't see him, but I knew who he was. He had haunted me for years. The voice belonged to that persistant caterpillar of Latin dance. He had the same nagging question to ask. The same question he had asked me so many times before. "Who are you?"

"Easy, I'm a wife and a mom," I replied.

"Is that all?" he asked.

"Isn't it enough?" I countered.

"Do you think it's enough?"

Ten years following the death of the Snowman, I'd become complacent in my life. "Yes. I think it is," I replied.

The caterpillar tipped upside-down from a branch overhead. Our faces nearly collided. Startled, I jumped backward. "Go away." I hissed.

"But, who are you?" he asked again as he clicked out a Tango beat with his castanets.

I rolled my eyes. "Humph," I sighed. "I told you. I am a wife and a mother. That should be enough," I replied.

"That is not who you are, but what you are."

"Leave me alone," I beseeched. I turned so I could no longer see him, and I continued to walk.

The caterpillar reappeared on the path directly in front of me. "I care not for the roles that you play in life. What I want to know is who are you?" He repeated.

"Leave———me———alone!" I yelled and I shooed him away with a wave.

He shook his head sadly:

"You have chosen not to heed my plea.
Thus I am forced to help thee see."

A single tear rolled down his pudgy face. He was gone.
"Good riddance!" I called after him.

CHAPTER 28

# PERFECT

My world was perfect. We had an acre lot nicely landscaped, a beautiful home and a healthy and happy four year old son. On top of all that, I was pregnant with our second child — a girl named Bryna Grace. Yes, everything was perfect — to me. I hadn't bothered to ask my husband how he felt about our new life.

When my husband and I met, I was a nonconformist — hell-bent I'd never marry, never have children and never again live in a small town. Now, at forty, I had all the trappings I vowed to avoid and worse yet, I loved it. I had changed. Becoming a mom changes a girl in ways she could never fathom. I fell madly in love with our son, with the joys of motherhood, with canning organic fruit and extolling the values of teaching sign-language to all toddlers.

By the time I noticed my husband's unhappiness he had been pushed far out to the fringes of my world. Left on the outside cold and alone, he wasn't sure he could stay. I couldn't blame him for wanting to go. I loved him. He loved me. Still, over the years life had gotten off balance until we weren't sure we could fix our marriage anymore. I sensed I was losing my husband. Along with him I sensed I was losing my world and my identity. An anxiety began to grow.

"Who are you?" the caterpillar's words demanded once more from the recesses of my mind.

*I don't know. I'm lost. I'm scared.* I felt sick to my stomach. My mouth watered. I swallowed hard. Probably just morning sickness, I reassured myself. I couldn't worry about a little morning sickness right now. Instead, while Gary took some German house guests to the O'Hare airport, I readied our place for an intimate gathering of family and friends.

Thinly sliced roast beef simmered in onions, au jus and mixed peppers. An unfamiliar, sticky wetness grew between my legs. I went to the upstairs bathroom. I forgot to lock the door. I pulled down my pants. Blood covered my panties — not the old, rusty kind that's okay when you're pregnant, but fresh blood, crimson red. In a panic I tried to clean it up. If I got rid of all traces then just maybe I could trick myself into believing that this wasn't happening.

I had forgotten to lock the door. Ethan let himself into the bathroom. "Momma, you're bleeding!" His face turned white.

I couldn't answer him. Instead I began to cry. Fear overtook him and he ran. He ran from the bathroom sobbing and screaming. "Help!" he screamed for anyone who would listen. "My mamma's bleeding! She's bleeding! Real bad! Oh, Mamma!" He ran back into the bathroom and stood with his hands outstretched in front of him wanting to hug me but afraid to touch me.

"I'm fine, Sweetheart," I reassured him as I quietly pulled my bloody clothes back up. I washed my hands. "All gone." I replied in a tender tone. I turned my hands over for him to inspect them. "See? All gone."

For a moment Ethan stood motionless and watched me. He searched my face to be sure I really meant what I said. I smiled calmly. I knelt down and hugged him. "Mommy's fine. See?" I nodded my head and looked in his eyes to set his mind at ease. I dried his tears with the sleeve of my blouse. While his eyes were closed I said, "Say moo cow."

He smiled, "Moooooooooo cow."

As his lips puckered into an exceptionally long moo, I kissed him. He opened his eyes and smiled. He began to relax.

"Now, let's go downstairs and call Grandma." I stood back up and held his hand. Together we slowly walked back downstairs. I called my mom, and in an unruffled voice I asked her to meet us at the doctor's office. She fired a barrage of questions toward me in rapid succession. I reminded her that Ethan was with me, and I promised to explain everything later at the doctor's office.

I'd almost forgotten guests would be arriving in less than an hour. I made the necessary calls to reschedule the party. I turned off the beef, grabbed my purse and together Ethan and I drove to the ob-gyn office twenty minutes away. As we sang Spanish children's songs to pass the time I realized that I had forgotten to change my clothes. *Oh well, the doctor will just have to deal with it,* I told myself as I silently pleaded for the life of my baby.

My mom's face brimmed with grief and worry as she met us at the door to the clinic. Nevertheless, she maintained her composure beautifully. I needed her to. At that moment her strength supported both of us.

"It's bad, Mom. Please don't hug me or anything. Not yet. I'm hanging on by the skin of my teeth here," I told her stiffly. I tried to smile.

She nodded and offered to take Ethan to the playground while I underwent a vaginal ultrasound. I will forever be grateful for her strength and for her patience, but most of all for the way she was able to put Ethan's needs before her own.

She placed an arm affectionately around his shoulders, and they walked slowly to her car. I stood in the doorway and watched until they disappeared from view. Then I counted slowly backward from five. When I reached zero I turned and entered the office.

I had never noticed before how many babies and pregnant women there are in an ob-gyn waiting room. I tried desperately not to resent each and every last one of them. Instead I concentrated on walking up to the desk and saying my name. That would take all of the fortitude I could muster. That accomplished, I sat down and waited for my turn to be seen.

While mom and Ethan played at the park, a kind, matronly obstetrician informed me that my baby's heart had stopped beating. Her nurse added, somewhat perplexed, that my blood pressure seemed quite high.

"Most often these things happen because genetically the baby is not healthy. It really is for the best," the doctor told me as we studied the ultrasound images of my lifeless baby.

She turned off the ultrasound machine and placed her hands on my knees. "Go ahead and get dressed. I'll be back in to discuss what to do next." She patted my knees and gently removed my feet from the stirrups.

I don't remember dressing. I vaguely remember a knock at the door. I looked up as the doctor re-entered the room and sat in a chair across from me. "These things happen in one out of every five pregnancies. The fetus was still relatively small. Small enough that I think we should let nature take its course. It's a healing process. You'll have some severe cramping, but that's good. Make an appointment to come back and see me in two weeks." She leaned over and patted the backs of my hands. "Take as long as you need," she said as she left the room.

I sat in that chair and wondered how was she to know that this was my last possibility at pregnancy — at another child? How was she to know that my husband was possibly leaving me? How was she to know that in the vacuum of impending divorce and miscarriage my identity was in crisis? How was she to know that my body as well as my mind would never willingly let my dead baby, Bryna go? How was she to know?

CHAPTER 29

# PONG TEA KOHN WALKING

Street vendors In Southeast Asia sell soft-boiled duck eggs with a partially developed duckling inside as food. In Cambodia they call these eggs pong tea khon. These partially developed ducklings are prized as particularly nutritious for pregnant women or those who have just given birth. For men they are considered an aphrodisiac.

In the weeks that followed the news that my baby's heart no longer beat, I became the vengeful mother spirit and protector of unsuccessful pregnancies everywhere. Pregnant women, those who had just given birth, and all men feared me. (Or at least I wanted them to.)

My abdomen continued to grow, but with death instead of life. Fever raged. I spent many hours on the cool tile floor seized by pain and cramping. Still my body refused to release Bryna's corpse.

Two weeks later, distended with infection and smelling of road-kill, I kept my appointment with the gynecologist who, two weeks earlier, I referred to as an obstetrician. I apologetically removed my bottoms. No amount of soap and water could censor the unpleasant aroma of decaying human flesh emanating from between my legs. I placed my feet once again in the stirrups. The doctor approached for a closer look.

After a full examination she removed her gloves and stood near my head. She looked worried. "I can't believe you can still walk. Do you think you can you get yourself over to the hospital? I'll call ahead. You need to be admitted."

"Now?" I puzzled. I didn't feel sick. I didn't feel —— anything.

"Right now! I have a few more patients to see. I'll meet you there as soon as I can get away."

We entered the deserted surgical area well after dark. As the cavernous room flickered to life in fluorescent hues of yellow, a nurse strapped me to a board; my arms spread perpendicular to my body like a crucifix. Although the doctor wanted to listen to Billy Joel, under the circumstances she let me choose the music. I picked jazz. She let out an audible sigh and tried to talk me into Billy Joel.

"No. Jazz," I reiterated dimly.

An oversized Russian man leaned over from behind my head. "Nice choice," he said, winking. His face was kind."Are you ready?" he asked.

I nodded.

He administered the anesthetic, and in a moment I was out. I don't recall much else from that evening. One of the saddest days of my life, and all I can remember is:

On a Wednesday, sometime after dark, in a large, cold room in the lower level of the hospital a sympathetic and motherly doctor ripped the decaying corpse of my baby from my body.

When I awoke, Bryna was gone. I was an empty shell.

I decorated my shell, as best I could, like an Easter egg—the kind they make in Poland. Outside I appeared intact and full of bright colors. Inside? Nothing. I let no one close. I let no one touch me for fear I would crack.

CHAPTER 30

# COATS

Three months later I dreamt I was a small child sleeping in a sea of coats on the guest bed at my grandparent's house.

When I was young, I begged to tag along to grown-up parties. I especially liked winter parties — the air outside so crisp and cold, inside a warm glow of laughter and merriment. Nearly everybody wore coats. I would enter the party and inhale deeply. The scent of stale smoke, booze and mixed pickles delighted my nose. I relished seeing sensible, women awkwardly teeter about in elegant shoes — their faces painted, their clothes starched and restrictive. I longed to see the men play cards and to eavesdrop on their colorful conversations. I didn't care to participate in the party. I didn't want to do the grown-up things; I just wanted to experience them with my senses. While they made merry, I wanted to smell and hear and watch.

As the guests arrived, their coats would be handed off to the coat handler — usually one of us kids held that honor. Ultimately the coats ended up thrown, willy-nilly onto the guest bed. If my parents were having a good time, they would eventually tell me to go in the guest bedroom and get some rest. I feigned disappointment, but secretly loved to climb into all of those coats. The fibers of the cloth mixed with the aroma of the lives the coats had lived. Some smelled stale and musty. Others smelled of exotic perfume and hair tonic. I inhaled deeply and pictured the houses the coats lived in. Some coats lived on farms. Some had house pets while others were made from the hides and furs of animals domestic and wild. Some deep-fried their food in old grease. I could smell something familiar. *Aha,* I remembered thinking, *somebody must be using a kerosene space heater. Like the one in our kitchen.* I smiled to myself.

When I was told to get some rest, rather than turning the lights on, I would feel my way through the textures of nubby cotton, scratchy wool and soft curly lamb. I'd burrow down, snuggle in and watch as the light danced around the room from the street below. I'd listen to the laughter and to the life. I felt safe there. Eventually I'd drift peacefully off to sleep floating in a sea of coats.

I awoke with a start back in my own room. The Snowman sat on the edge of my bed. Before he even spoke I knew it was him. The unmistakable aroma of Brut and Brylcreem flooded the room.

"Are you going to be all right?" he asked.

Logically, I knew he couldn't be real. He died many years ago. Still, the sound of his voice brought a glimmer of joy to my dark and hostile heart. I didn't care if he was a figment of my imagination. I teetered on the edge like Humpty Dumpty on the wall. I just wanted him to stay. I wanted him to walk beside me through my life. Visit my home. Meet my Ethan. He couldn't. He was dead. Still, he was here now. Or was he? I can't say. All I know for sure is that his presence gripped me in delighted heartbreak.

"Your mom made you some Jell-O," he said.

The Snowman came back from the grave to tell me that my mom had made Jell-O. I shook my head in disbelief.

If the Snowman vanished, I'd fall off the edge and crack into a million pieces. I'd be lost forever in the pockets of the coats from winters past. I continued to face away from him. "What kind?" I asked.

"Oh, that one with the little canned oranges and the cottage cheese."

I squeezed my eyes shut and turned up my nose. (That's not my favorite kind of Jell-O. I wanted lime Jell-O – with pears in it.)

"Please stay," I silently pleaded.

I knew my mom was worried about me. When she worried, she cooked.

At a dead Snowman's suggestion of Jell-O, I felt —— if not hungry at least able to eat.

"Did she make any green Jell-O with pears in it?" I asked.

"I'm not sure," the Snowman said as he set a hand on my hip.

I could feel the weight of it. I turned to look at him. He looked old and troubled. I lay my head in his lap. He stroked my hair. Neither of us spoke another word. I fell back asleep.

In the morning I could feel my icy blood warm, thaw and slowly seep back into my veins — first into my chest, beginning to strengthen me. I felt relief. I stopped cursing life, God, the fates, the universe.

*Tears are the silent language of grief.*

———— Voltaire

CHAPTER 31

# SURVIVING

I awoke to find my life in shambles. With Bryna gone and my marriage in jeopardy, I had numbly existed. I can't say for how long. Time has no meaning when you're asleep. When I finally awoke, I wanted my life back.

Regardless of my marital status, regardless of my ability to ever have another child, I wanted more than anything to live. I just had to figure out how. I was scared. Trapped in a cage I built myself, I paced. In my pacing I could find no way out. I needed some help. I called the doctor. She was with another patient. I began to exercise — hard. When I finally reached complete exhaustion, I took a nap. When I awoke I ate some cold chicken.

Four hours later the doctor returned my call. I let the answering machine take it. Somewhere between the exercise, the nap and the cold chicken I found the strength to make it through another day. I discovered if I kept myself physically exhausted and partially starved, I had no energy left to think. My newfound mindlessness made my existence bearable. So that became my routine.

I found I liked it that way. In time my grief caught up with me.

I squeezed in a ten-hour-a-day-job as a landscaper. The increased physical exhaustion numbed my mind and promoted dreamless sleep. I mechanically filled the roles of my life. I needed to.

I had a four-year-old son who needed his mom. I had a home and a garden. I had a marriage in need of repair.

I was still in love with my husband. I felt we should be together forever, but I was too sick, too tired and too grief-stricken to fight. I reluctantly offered Gary the freedom he requested.

Funny thing is, when I finally let him go, he decided to stay. We didn't divorce. We worked it out and life went on.

My body continued — on a treadmill — inside a cage — where everything was cold, damp and gray.

My spirit sat down in a drab, over-stuffed chair in the foyer and stared blankly at two doors and a box.

Edna June grabbed her doctor's bag and headed off in my direction.

It would take me nearly two years to realize she had come. It would take me another two years to admit it.

*And the Devil did grin for his darling sin*
*Is pride that apes humility*

——————— Samuel Taylor Coleridge

CHAPTER 32

# PITY

N early four years had passed since I initially sat down in the foyer and nearly six months since I stepped off of the treadmill. Christmas was right around the corner. I had two surgeries behind me. I would not have to start radiation until the first of the year. On top of that, I received a wonderful gift from Hermes. I tore open the envelope and read the card. It stated:

> *Dear Kristine,*
> *You've completed your infusions. The yew has nourished your soul well. You may pick-up your body at the oncologist's office at your earliest convenience.*
> *In honor of the strength you've conveyed during the past months, I wish to also give back that which is yours. You've proven yourself worthy. Nice work.*
>
> > *Sincerely,*
> > *Hermes*

I tore into my present. Inside the beautifully wrapped package, tucked between two pale-pink pieces of tissue paper, rested my neatly folded mind.

I felt whole again. "Let's go to Chicago, downtown, and see the lights," I begged my husband. "And let's take the train." I had the urge to experience a full-blown, commercialized, American Christmas complete with Nuremberg-style Christkindlmarket, decorated storefronts and holiday cheer. I knew it would be crisp and cold, crowded and Christmassy and I wanted to experience every facet.

We drove to Harvard, Illinois, and caught the Metrarail train downtown to Ogilvie Station. The storefronts sparkled with ribbons and bows. Macy's picked up the flagship torch from Marshall Fields' fallen hands. The Green Bay Packers played the Chicago Bears at Soldier Field. The streets buzzed with holiday shoppers, hungry hawkers and the homeless.

We visited the Millennium Bean. We watched the ice skaters glide around in circles. We shopped the colorful booths, where thickly accented vendors hawked wares from all over the world. We drank mulled wine and ate hearty German fare. We posed for pictures with a street musician and his scorching saxophone. Although he never asked, we dropped a few bucks in his instrument case. Many others on the street, however, did ask us for spare change.

"Why do those people keep asking us for money?" Ethan asked.

"They're homeless," I replied without giving much thought to what I had just said.

"They have no place to live?" His eyes widened in disbelief.

"I'm sure that's not entirely true," I assured him.

"How do we know who really needs our help?" Ethan asked wanting to help them all.

"We don't."

Ethan continued to push. He pitied them. Pity was something I had become quite familiar with in the past six months. Anger began to smolder and rise from my belly.

"How can I not feel sorry for them?" Ethan asked and looked up at me. He could tell I was angry. Still his heart ached for the many people he now believed had no homes. In an attempt to understand, he willingly placed himself in the path of my smoldering anger.

"Pity doesn't put food in their stomachs, Ethan!" I rebuked through clenched teeth. I remembered the dark cloud that passed through the Snowman's face as he said the word *pity* so many years before. Now, I understood his resentment.

I took a deep breath and quieted my growing rage. I searched for words to help an eight-year-old-boy understand pity from the other side.

"If you pity someone," I began, "you're, at the very least, judging him from your perspective. Worse yet, you may in fact, be dumping your own negative baggage on somebody who's already down-and-out. You know what I mean?"

"No." Ethan shook his head. I could see in his eyes that he still longed to save the world, or at the very least, the Chicago homeless.

"Sweetheart, if you feel moved to give somebody a helping hand then do it. If you don't... then don't. Respect people's choices for what they are and, above all, do not pity anyone. Pity is not nice. It is not helpful. It makes people feel like crap!" And with that I closed the conversation on pity.

For a moment, Ethan considered pushing the issue one more time. Thankfully, he decided against it.

I knelt down beside him. I held his face in my hands. "E, you are so kind and caring. I hope you never change."

As I looked at his innocent face, I knew that I couldn't understand pity, not until I became a forty-something-year-old cancer patient. *He's just a kid. How could I expect him to understand?* I reminded myself.

"Never stop caring. Just try to remember that caring and pity are not the same. Someday, you'll get it, okay?" I attempted to reassure him.

He nodded and I kissed his eyelids.

The sun moved behind the skyscrapers and a polar wind cut us through to the bone. We walked briskly back to Ogilvie Station and boarded the next train bound for Harvard. We sat in the balcony and watched as the train filled with passengers to overflowing.

The rival football game was over, and fans from both sides streamed onto the train. A gang of rowdy firefighters sat alongside us. As the northbound train bumped along, the youngest fireman fell asleep next to me. Halfway through the ride, he awoke and staggered toward the bathroom. When he returned, the front of his shirt was visibly stained and he reeked of vomit. His buddies wheedled and teased. He smiled smugly; and, without warning, he fire-hosed Chicago-Red-Hots and beer all over my brand-new snow boots. My all-American, Chicago Christmas was complete.

Life is messy. No longer were my snow boots pristine and pretty. They too had experienced Christmas. They too had experienced Chicago. They too had experienced life.

Before I close this chapter, I'd like to offer one last note on pity. Life is temporary. Circumstances are temporary. The best we can do for the people of this world is to show them unbiased respect. Greet the very best in all people. Don't ignore them; don't treat them as though they are invisible. Don't pity them. If you can help, help. If not, I kind word and a genuine smile can be priceless.

We cannot begin to know the circumstances surrounding another person's life, even if we've walked many miles in her vomit-covered snow boots.

CHAPTER 33

# THE RIDE

Although I enjoyed our trip to Chicago, as I scraped dried-on firefighter puke from my snow boots, I vowed to take my dream car the next time.

My perfect car would have: the reliability of a Volvo 240; the two-tone leather seats of a Mazda Speed 6; the ability to tell me exactly how many miles I can go before I run out of gas like the Audi A6; and it'd be a station wagon — nice and tall in the back for hauling plants — like a hearse. The middle console compartment would be deep enough to park a moped in — like the Acura MDX. My car would be fast with heated seats and a sun roof. Did I mention the color? Wasabi green! Oh yeah, and it would have 87 cup holders.

I need drinks — lots and lots of drinks — some hot and some cold. My husband needs drinks, and my son, he needs drinks too.

Some drinks would be full. Some empty. Some older beverages would no doubt have begun to sprout hair. Even they need a place to rest, lest they spew moldy juice all over my tangerine, shag floor mats.

Ethan brought home a book from the school library the other day. Back in the 1960s mopeds sporting a superfluity of rear-view mirrors were all the rage. Does anyone really need a moped with 21 mirrors? How about 33? I'm not sure. I never used a moped as my primary mode of transportation. But a vehicle with 87 cup holders, I can personally attest to the probability of a practical and nearly mandatory use of every glorious one. I'd like them of varying sizes, shapes and depths. Some would be for... well... cups, some for silos.

One particularly hot and balmy day I discovered, purely by accident, that a large beverage from a fast-food chain comes in, of all things, a silo. I'm pretty sure the side surface of my beverage storage tower of ice and tea was emblazoned with the Harvestore name and emblem.

"Where is a cup holder large enough to house one of those bad boys?" I ask you. My dream car would have one. No, it would have three.

And, since I'm on the subject, why don't most cup holders come with a slot for the cup handle? My Tinker Bell go-mug won't fit in a standard cup holder. Yeah, I could take the plain silver go-mug, but my coffee doesn't taste as good out of that one.

Although not actually for cups, I'll need at least five square and three rectangle cup holders. I'd like space for my cell phone, three small notebooks, scraps of paper, receipts, addresses, phone numbers (even though I forgot to write down to whom the number belongs) and my mini tape recorder. The pink cup holders should be rather small and shallow to hold spare change and hair doodads. Lastly, I'll need a tall, skinny cup holder for pens and pencils.

I love my ideal car; the only problem is that I can't find it anywhere. Trust me, my husband has diligently tried. This past February I told him, "just because I want something and say so, doesn't mean you have to try to get it for me."

He threw his hands in the air in exasperation. "Why couldn't you have mentioned that seventeen years ago?" he exclaimed.

"I thought you knew," I said with a shrug.

Until my ultimate driving machine is invented, I drive what I drive.

In all honesty, most days I don't give it a second thought. As long as I get from point A to point B and back again, I'm happy. That's the real key to cars and to life.

I could sit in my car and admire the parts I love. I could sit in my car and pine away for the parts I find lacking. Instead I crank it over. I start my engine, and I get moving. I roll down the window. I feel the cool wind on my face as I push the accelerator. I'm able to get to where I'm going and back.

In order to help with that, I got a GPS. Initially it charted a 104 mile round-trip course to my radiation treatments. It tried to tell me where to go. I'm a woman. I know better than some little computer gismo how to get to where I'm going. The GPS suggested a route. Yes, it was just a suggestion. And it was wrong. I manually manipulated the machine with via points, alternate routes and any other way possible to get the GPS to choose my way. Because I knew my way had to be right — exclusively right.

During my six weeks of radiation treatments I experimented with a variety of routes. The time variance between the shortest and the longest route turned out to be **four minutes**. *What a revelation!* I discovered I could choose between seven or eight different paths and barring any road blocks, accidents or traffic jams, I would arrive within four minutes of any other path.

I began to choose on preference instead of efficiency. It helped make the journey to an unpleasant destination more bearable, occasionally bordering on enjoyable. I've since adopted the same philosophy in life.

As you go through your life, chances are the path you choose will have advantages and disadvantages, and so will your mode of transportation. Efficiency is overrated. My advice, for what it's worth, is to enjoy the ride. If you're not, override your GPS by any means possible. Recalculate. The additional time it costs will seem inconsequential compared to the amount of pleasure you'll experience on your new path.

For now, I'm hungry. I search the GPS Points of Interest for pizza — wood fired pizza. I set a pizza via point on my route planner, put on my sun glasses, crank Axel F on the radio and head for home — only 29 more radiation treatments to go — and counting.

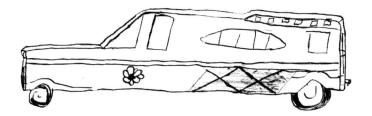

*With each passage of human growth*
*we must shed a protective structure*
*(like a hardy crustacean).*
*We are left exposed and vulnerable –*
*but yeasty and embryonic again,*
*capable of stretching in ways*
*we hadn't known before.*

——— Gail Sheehy

CHAPTER 34

# NAKED CRAB

Cold tremors of vulnerability raced up my spine. I recalled the comfort I felt many moons ago in a suburban sweat-lodge north of San Francisco. I begged my husband for a sauna. Like a hermit crab, I would use the sauna as a kind of borrowed shell until I grew some thicker skin. My radiologist sadly had other ideas. Until completely finished with treatments, I was barred from the sauna. I shivered as I waited.

Finally the day arrived. Radiation was over. I enter the sauna for the first time. I placed a CD called *The Blues, Naturally* into the sound system. The CD combined soothing sounds of nature with blues music. I left all of the lights off. The darkness and the heat enveloped me as the music soothed my weary soul. I felt safe. For the first time in months, I relaxed. My body, however, refused to sweat.

Raw emotion welled up. *The worst is over.* Pensively, I began to cry. The initial tears broke through my stoic façade. The floodgates opened and the tears turned to uncontrollable sobs. I no longer tried to hold them back.

As the sauna held me in a safe embrace, the tears washed away my anguish and my pain. Eventually the sauna, as well as my tears, turned off. I sat for another twenty minutes. I stretched, took a cold shower and began to grow my new skin.

CHAPTER 35

## HEADACHES AND PROBABILITIES

I was down to the easy part (or so I thought). All I had left to do was to take a tiny white pill every morning for five years. Over the course of treatment I learned that, even without my ovaries, my body may still find a way to produce estrogen. I learned that some foods can also produce estrogen. I learned that my type of cancer feeds on estrogen and; therefore, I became acquainted with a little white pill called Arimidex — the estrogen inhibitor.

Oh, but for the love of estrogen my body yearned and my head throbbed as that first dose entered my bloodstream. I had a mind-splitting headache — nearly every day, that became the norm. My head throbbed and my eyes blurred from the pain, but, I had a smorgasbord of pain remedies at my disposal. Most days I'd head straight to the medicine cabinet where I'd begin with the letter "A" (acetaminophen, Advil or aspirin) depending on my mood. Realizing that too much pain medication was probably not particularly healthy, I decided one day to try some nice soothing home remedies instead of painkillers. I began with an organic blend of peppermint tea laced with honey and lemon. I followed that up with cold packs to my forehead, my eyes and the back of my neck. Followed in rapid succession by heat, followed by cold, followed by skull-cracking pain that no painkiller could ease. I'd waited too long and now even the slightest change in pressure made it feel like my brains would push through the backs of my eyeballs causing them to spill out onto our dusty rose carpeting.

"Honey!" I called to my husband. "Call the doctor I think I'm going to die!"

My husband moved for the phone.

"Honey!" I pleaded weaker this time, "Bring me two Excedrin Migraines and an espresso with sugar!"

Gary dropped the phone and dashed to the kitchen before returning with two tablets and a cup of coffee.

I took the aspirin. I drank the strong, black, sweet coffee. I waited. The pain continued to grow until it became nearly unbearable and certainly unforgettable.

I rolled around on the floor. No relief. I crawled toward the basement stairs – afraid to stand. The pressure inside my head was greater than the ambient air pressure. I headed for lower ground; perhaps I could gain some relief where the air was thicker. As I crawled over the sea of wall-to-wall pinkness I thought, *we really need to update our early 1990s décor, but not today.* I crossed the threshold into the kitchen. *Ah,* I rested my cheek against the cool, soothing, cornflower-blue linoleum. I'd almost reached the stairs.

"Honey!" I yelled — the sound of my own voice had become too painful to tolerate, "Narcotics stat. And Coca Cola."

"Vicodin or Darvon?" He asked as he sprinted up the stairs to the medicine cabinet on the second floor where I kept the big guns.

"Surprise me."

He returned in a flash.

I washed down some more pills with warm Coke. My temperature swung like a manic pendulum between near-spontaneous combustion and frigid tremors. I wondered if this is how a heroin addict felt while in the throes of the DTs. I missed my estrogen. I missed it emotionally, psychologically and physically. I craved it, but Cancer craved it more. If I gave her some, she'd become stronger so instead I slinked into the basement and poured myself into the sauna.

I crumpled up on the floor of the sauna shivering, sweating, moaning, boiling and writhing in pain. Vicodin, espresso, Darvon, aspirin and Coca Cola coursed through my veins. Still, no relief. I wondered if the combination of various medications swimming in Coke and coffee was wise or deadly. *Too late now,* I guessed.

Gary joined me in the basement with a doctor on the line. The oncologist-on-call assured me that the cocktail of drugs and drinks I took wouldn't kill me. In fact he suggested I throw down another Vicodin or two until I experienced relief.

"No one should have to face the next five years with a headache," he empathized. He then recommended I stop taking the Arimidex until we could determine what was causing the headaches. I don't think the doctor-on-call realized that I had my ovaries removed in order to qualify for this cancer inhibiting drug that would otherwise be off-limits to me.

I lay in the sauna and contemplated going off my medication. That would mean that I had my ovaries removed for nothing. I didn't like that option. I rummaged around for an alternative I could live with. Way back in the dark recesses of my mind filed under the letter "C", I uncovered an alleviating concept — something I learned in sophomore grammar class — the difference between continual and continuous. That difference made this and all subsequent headaches tolerable.

Even if I had continual headaches I was relatively sure that they would not be continuous. Therefore, I didn't have to face five years of headaches. If I lived my life a moment at a time, I would experience moments when I would no longer be suffering yesterday's headache and tomorrow's headache would not have come yet.

As for today, I've writhed in various degrees of pain from 4:30

PM until 1:30 AM. I then slept well until 5 AM. When I awoke, the headache, if not gone, was greatly diminished.

Twenty-seven days later, I lived a complete twenty-four hours with no headache. That morning I lingered in bed soaking in the sweet sense of pain-free lounging. I didn't worry or even think about the possible pain of later that day nor did I waste the preciousness of that moment recalling the pain of headaches past. For that moment my brow widened and relaxed.

Would I have a headache later that day? Probably. (In fact, I did.) But I had learned that when dealing with pain, as when facing death, it's best to throw probabilities to the wind. Pain and death just are. There's no way to prepare for the siege. Instead I worked to enjoy the time on either side of both.

What's *The Upside Of Down*? Life is lived in moments. I learned to experience my life frame by frame. I purposefully cut out snippets of time for fun, laughter, pampering, observing the wonders of life and enjoying time with those I love. I diced up my days and built pretty borders around them. The good ones I placed in my pockets and carried with me. The bad ones I endured knowing they wouldn't last forever. Also, procrastination was forced to take a backseat. When I felt good, I took advantage of the time I'd been given.

Lastly, I learned to appreciate my time away from the pain. Compared to death, a headache is a minor setback. (Yes, even a really bad headache.) For the first year, I took some aspirin or a Vicodin and I got on with living.

One year and countless headaches later I found an alternate way to manage my headaches back under the letter "A" — acupuncture. After my first treatment my headaches began to subside in frequency and severity. Dr. Chi, my acupuncturist, suggested adding Tui Na massage. The new approach treated my whole body. The circulation in my hands and feet improved. My eyes became whiter and less dry. I, all of me, felt better, healthier.

*The whole course of things goes to teach us faith.*
*We need only obey.*

———— Emerson

CHAPTER 36

## SAVANNAH EASTER

I became Schrödinger's cat: I existed both dead and alive until I met, once again, with the oncologist. His observation would decide whether the barrage of prescribed treatments had worked or not.

Since I wasn't entirely sure of the outcome, I decided I'd like to spend Easter in Savannah, Georgia, dubbed the most haunted city in America. I wished to commune with both the living and the dead.

Easter week arrived, and we caught a plane. Ethan packed his own luggage. Just to be safe, I asked, "E-man, you all packed?"

"Yup," he replied.

"Let's go through your suitcase together, just to be sure?"

"Okay, I have my wind-up bug named Sparky, my voice changer, my manta ray, Jeffrey Ford-the super bug — with remote control — and my swim goggles."

"Can you think of anything else you might need to bring?" I asked hoping he'd add underwear and a toothbrush to the list.

"Oh yeah, I should bring my finger guillotine, my Zeebeez Mega Bounce and my water-squirting calculator."

I helped him add a few necessities to his luggage and I snuck my New Webster's Pocket Dictionary into his carry-on. I knew he wouldn't mind.

Soon we arrived in warm, sunny Savannah.

At 500 West Charlton Street, I lay in an unfamiliar bed with a mind-splitting headache — the tenth one in as many days. The sun had just begun to stream through the curtains. I remembered how much I used to love the sun. Now I wrapped the pillow tightly around my head to shade my eyes. The white crisp linens smelled faintly of bleach. Unable to sleep yet shunning the light, I composed an imaginary letter to my doctor wherein I detailed the life and times of a cancer patient – of this cancer patient:

> *Dear Doc,*
> *Before you told me I was sick, I felt fine, better than fine.*
> *How could cancer have been eating away at me when I*
> *felt so good? Your treatments are what have zapped my life*
> *force and left me old, tired and sick…*

*Ugh!*

I rolled my head up tighter inside the pillow. *It's futile,* I told myself. What's done is done.

I rolled onto my other side. *Still, does he have a clue what really goes on inside my body and my head?* I wondered. *Does he even care? Would he be surprised to learn that the dream of thriving had become a distant memory? Would he care to learn the tricks I'd adopted just to get through a day?*

*Grrrrrr.* I tossed the pillow at the window and curled up in a ball.

Ethan, too, noticed the golden glow of dawn. Unlike me, he embraced it. He ran on tiptoes up to the east-facing window of our hotel room and tore open the drapes. The streets below buzzed with big-city hustle and bustle. Thrilled that morning had finally arrived, he didn't want to miss a moment of it. On the street below, the police had cordoned off the Spring Hill Redoubt. It appeared that the site of the Siege of Savannah, one of the bloodiest battles of the Civil War, had claimed another life. However, in the pale early morning the guns were once again silent, and Ethan lost interest in the hubbub below.

He pulled an easy chair up to the window, taped a piece of paper to the glass and began to draw. As his picture grew in detail and understanding of depth and shadow, he hummed a happy tune. I realized it was the same one playing quietly inside my head. *Had we heard it somewhere? Were our radios tuned to the same frequency?*

*Come on, Old Girl.* I chided myself. *It's dawn — a new day.* I slunk from the bed to the shower. Semi-revived by water and steam, I packed my aching carcass into one of the few remaining outfits I owned that still fit. Together Gary, Ethan and I headed downstairs where we nourished our bodies with waffles and fresh fruit, coffee and juice. Some food in my belly I numbed my hormone-deficient hangover with a Vicodin, or was it two? I placed a large-brimmed hat atop my head and hid my sagging, yellow eyes behind dark sunglasses. Under a cloudless, blue sky, Savannah, Georgia, Vitamin D and vibrant health awaited me. "Good morning, world!" I exclaimed unenthusiastically as I pulled the brim of my hat down lower.

*Emotion is the chief source of all becoming-conscious.*
*There can be no transforming of darkness into light*
*and of apathy into movement without emotion.*

——— Carl Jung

CHAPTER 37

## EMOTIONS AND MENOPAUSE

Edna June had come into my life to shake things up and get things moving. In an acquaintance and initiation ceremony to my emotions, Edna sacrificed my ovaries effectively giving my emotions super powers. Women throughout the ages have made the epic leap from child-bearer to crone, mine required a scalpel.

I experienced puberty in reverse and it's not for sissies. Hailed most often as The Change, you and I know it as menopause. When it comes right down to it, I only have one piece of advice: Learn how to swim in an ever changing sea of emotions before you dive in. If you're over forty and a woman, start practicing now. Oh, and learn how to breathe. (Okay, I admit it, that's two pieces of advice.) As the emotions attempt to take over, exhale methodically through your nose and ride it out — right-side up, upside-down, it doesn't matter.

As I practiced the exhale, my mind chewed on the word emotion. Emotion. *E + motion. What's the E for? Does E stand for evoke? Do emotions evoke motion? Motion. E-Motion. Locomotion. Movement. Moved. Moved by music. Moved to tears. How come I never noticed the motion in emotion before?*

My eyes sprang open as Emotion swallowed me up and spit me out onto the floor of a Savannah hotel room at three o'clock in the morning. Emotion wasn't leaving until I discovered what Noah Webster had to say about it. (Emotions are vain that way.)

Left with no choice, I rifled through my purse looking for my pocket dictionary; it wasn't there. I looked in my Pendleton bag. *Nope, not there either.* I wasn't really in the mood to hunt for a dictionary at this time of the morning, but *emotion* insisted. I stuck a small flashlight under my chin and dug around the hotel room with both hands.

Finally I found the dictionary inside my suitcase stacked up with a bunch of brochures on Savannah and some clothes that were too clean to throw in with the dirty laundry, but too dirty to fold. *Emotion* cuffed me upside the head. I regained my focus. I pushed the clothes out of the way, snatched up the dictionary and thumbed through it until I reached the entry dedicated to *emotion.*

According to Webster *emotion* comes from the Latin words *emovere* or *emotum* which means to move, to shake, or to stir up. My dictionary went on to define *emotion* in two ways: First as a migration — a movement from one place to another, secondly as an agitation, a disturbance or tumultuous movement, whether physical or social. In other words, *Emotion* is the mover and shaker in life.

I didn't like where I was. Not physically, not mentally, not spiritually. I didn't yet know where I was heading. Emotion could and would guide my migration, but first I had to learn how to follow its lead. Instead of sinking under the weight of my emotions, I practiced surfing the sensational waves.

Sometimes my deep seated emotional stirrings made me wonder if I'd gone mad. I decided, instead of freaking-out, I'd embrace my emotional crazies. I pined for the closeness of others on the edge. "Let's go to Clary's for breakfast," I said as I rubbed my hands together in anticipation. "Oh, and let's stop off at the Gryphon Tea Room. I want to see the Tiffany glass ceiling," I added.

As we walked the streets of Savannah's historic district on our way to the Gryphon Room, I soaked in the beauty of this antebellum city. The sky shown in muted hues of blue and lavender. The azalea blossoms seemed to pop open spontaneously as we walked by. The mosquitoes, thankfully, hadn't yet bloomed. The air hung humid and heavy, but not yet hot. I walked along extolling the beauty of Savannah and the landscape that surrounded me. Ethan turned to Gary and said, "I'll betcha my allowance that Mama will cry when she sees the Tiffany ceiling."

Gary nudged him and whispered back, "Listen to her. I'll bet you she doesn't make it past the next square."

Incidentally, Ethan won the bet. I made it to the Gryphon Tea Room before an emotional wave of joy and beauty brought tears to my eyes.

*Tough and funny and a little bit kind:*
*that is as near to perfection*
*as a human being can be.*

————— Mignon McLaughlin

CHAPTER 38

# CLARY'S CAFE

If you've ever read, *Midnight in the Garden of Good and Evil,* you'll recall that while in Savannah the author, John Berendt, began his mornings at Clary's Cafe. He went for breakfast, but more for the colorful patrons. In my present state, I too longed for breakfast at Clary's. I wasn't disappointed. Just as I'd hoped, we had the good fortune of communing with a charming woman from the emotional edge.

We arrived late by breakfast standards, but early for lunch. We sat at the counter. A dark-haired woman in her late 30s stood behind us. She slowly circled back and forth hoping someone would make eye contact. My stomach tickled in anticipation. Ethan turned around, gave her an apprehensive wave and said, "Hi."

She was unique. But then, I like that in a person. *Is she stalking us? I wondered. Is she crazy? Maybe, but what's the difference between crazy, and just a little zany or eccentric? I'll take that over normal any day.*

ℰℭ

Like ghosts, folks on the fringe use children as their in. Children have no preconceived notions of social order. A child will talk to a homeless man, a movie star, the queen, a cockroach, a dead person, his own reflection and a tree all with the same enthusiasm. At school the next day, which one will make the most fascinating story to tell his friends? My vote is for the cockroach or the crow Ethan spoke to while on vacation.

As Gary stood inside at a car rental counter and signed the paper work for a mid-sized car, Ethan and I went outside and chose our ride. We picked a blue Ford Fusion.

"Mama," Ethan turned to me and said, "People think crows are stupid, but he's not dumb." He pointed over my shoulder. "He's a shape shifter."

I turned to see a crow sitting on top of a silver Hyundai Sonata. *Oh, here we go,* I thought to myself.

Ethan, who had been straddling the hump in the back with his feet, while his upper body jutted over the center armrests, turned and sat down on the console facing backward. "He has a broken leg. He's tired and hungry." Ethan looked at the crow as he spoke. "Do you have anything he could eat?"

"I have a tangerine," I offered. "Perhaps that'll give him the strength he needs to shift back. What was he, anyway?"

Ethan didn't answer. He looked at me as if to say, "A human, you moron," but he knew better than to take that tone with me. "He doesn't like tangerines, Mama."

"Here, crow." I threw two segments of tangerine on the ground next to the Sonata. The crow didn't budge. Instead, he looked directly at me with a penetrating, black stare.

"Mom!" Ethan reprimanded as he buried his face in his hands, "I told you! He doesn't like tangerines!" The crow hobbled from the Sonata on one good leg and disappeared into a hedge.

ॐﱠᲜ

Back at Clary's, the dark-haired stranger took Ethan's gesture to mean that the floodgates of conversation were now officially open.

As she spoke, we ate our breakfast. She didn't seem to care much if we talked. It was more important to her that we listened — and listen we did. Occasionally we nodded politely or smiled. Gary tried in vain to interject an occasional tidbit from our travels into the conversation. She didn't seem to notice. She preferred our silence. We took turns randomly spicing up our nonverbal replies with glances of shock or dismay.

As she entertained us with her mesmerizing tales, three separate waitresses asked if we needed *anything*. They drew out the word *anything* as they each, in turn, glared at our storyteller. Their eyes betrayed the offer to bounce the dark-haired stranger from the premises. She politely awaited her fate. We wanted her to stay. Her melodrama resumed. I admired her stamina – her free-flowing energy and over-the-top antics. She embodied the wonderful opposite of apathy.

We discovered that our dark-haired storyteller loved to watch television. It appeared that throughout the years she spent many days in front of TVs around the world — most recently in New Zealand. She didn't have much good to report on New Zealand. By all reports, New Zealand television is "vulgar, senseless and full of nudity and other horrible atrocities no self-respecting American would be caught dead watching".

Once she heard herself say the word *dead* an interesting shift occurred in the conversation. She stopped talking for a moment and moved in close. We all stopped chewing. We even stopped breathing. She glanced from side to side to see if anyone was eavesdropping.

"Do you realize that this whole city is built on dead people?" she whispered. Her face contorted in a strange way. When her eyes met mine, a shiver trickled down my spine, and I dropped my fork.

She watched us for many moments, then physically took one step backward and verbally stepped right back into her dissertation on New Zealand: "They have the best volcanic soil in New Zealand. You can grow anything there. It's so good, you can plant a dead person and he will come back to life! I mean it, wonderful soil." She smiled and clicked her heels. With that our twenty-minute one-sided conversation sadly ended.

What an amazing adventure at a breakfast counter on a warm and wonderful Savannah Wednesday. We paid our bill and breezed off arm-in-arm-in-arm. Our eyes and hearts open to the outlandish, the eccentric, the peculiar and the bizarre.

CHAPTER 39

# DOLDRUMS

Our encounter at Clary's blew wind in our sails and kept us from the Doldrums. The dark-haired stranger had, in effect, jammed an oar down our throats and given our waters an emotional stir. Life needs a stir every now and then.

I just had to hear what Noah Webster had to say about the Doldrums. I pulled my pocket dictionary from my purse. Therein Noah defined the *Doldrums* as a mental disturbance, low spirits, as confused or stupid. He followed up the initial definition with four varying examples of the *Doldrums*:

1. A dullard. A sluggish person.
2. Dullness, depression, the dumps.
3. A part of ocean near the equator abounding in calms, squalls and light, baffling winds which sometimes prevent all progress.
4. A state of listlessness, ennui, tedium.

In any long-term project, whether raising kids, going to college or writing a book, I've experienced the Doldrums. And when I do, I want to throw up my hands and quit. Marriage is no exception.

Marriage is designed for support in times of adventure, danger or hardship. Most extreme expeditions advise using the buddy system for safety. A dive partner — someone to count on if your regulator gets stuck — is essential in SCUBA diving. Mountain climbers have climbing partners. The buddy system for the extreme expedition called life — is marriage.

I'm going to go out on a limb here and suggest that most, if not all marriages, go through the Doldrums — more than once. When it happens we all want to quit. Marriage cannot survive the Doldrums indefinitely. Often after years in the Doldrums, one or the other partner, out of boredom or despair, begins to make waves. Sometimes waves, although painful and scary, represent the best hope for escaping. If you find yourself stuck, adrift, going nowhere, chart a course to… anywhere, perhaps Clary's for breakfast. Begin to paddle with whatever you have. Use a teaspoon if that's all you've got.

It is usually wise, however, in any marriage to keep in mind the acute differences between men and women. As we left Clary's we strolled past Christopher's on East Liberty. There we crossed paths with a woman wearing three-inch stiletto heels. "How does she walk in those shoes?" I asked my husband.

"Honey, her dress is see-through. I didn't even realize she was wearing shoes," he replied. Ethan covered his eyes. He parted his fingers just enough to get an eyeful. I have a sneaking suspicion that he didn't notice she was wearing shoes either.

*For lack of an occasional expression of love,*
*a relationship strong at the seams can wear thin in the middle.*

———— Robert Brault

*The echo began in some indescribable way to undermine her hold on life. Coming at a moment when she chanced to be fatigued, it had managed to murmur, "Pathos, piety, courage – they exist, but are identical, and so is filth. Everything exists, nothing has value." If one had spoken vileness in that place or quoted lofty poetry, the comment would have been the same – "ou-boum". Existing in apathy – we become the echo removed from the original.*

——— Edward Morgan Forester

CHAPTER 40

# HEALTHY, WEALTHY AND WISE

The Georgia coast offers two full weeks of fabulous bug-free weather a year — one in April and the other in late October. The good weather gods smiled on us. We had picked the perfect week this spring. Although we headed off in no particular direction with no particular place to go, we refused to waste a minute of this glorious day indoors, and so we walked. We passed an old woman sitting at a large, wooden table in her front yard.

"Do you notice my table?" she asked as she waved an arthritic hand in an exaggerated sweep over the table's surface.

I wanted to pretend not to hear her. I wanted to keep walking, but my legs refused to take another step. I turned to face her. "It's very nice," I lied through a painted-on smile. In reality, her table looked plain, dingy. Still I nodded pleasantly. "I don't care for any ———— readings." I told her, although she never asked if I did.

With her hands she drew my attention back to her table. "It has four legs," she continued.

"Uh huh," I replied and nodded again more emphatically this time, hoping to hide my inner judgments of her and her table.

The old woman leaned hard on the corner of her table and she stood. Standing, she looked much smaller and older than I'd expected. She couldn't have been more than five feet tall, yet she reminded me of an oak tree, a scrub oak gnarled, burled and somehow stunted by time and fate. Her spine twisted in an unnatural arc as she walked. She slowly crossed toward the sidewalk. "My table." She patted it gently. "It does not wobble." She didn't make eye contact but pulled out a chair and motioned for me to sit. I did.

As I sat down, she paused for a moment with her back to me and leaned on her table. She wore a wool, knee-length, black, A-line skirt and thick, black stockings over stout, bowed legs. I couldn't help but notice that one of her legs appeared substantially shorter than the other. Her hip protruded unnaturally in order to pick up the slack. She slowly returned to her seat behind the table. "Yes. All four legs are perfectly balanced," she said as she leaned forward and gave me a deeply penetrating gaze.

Many thoughts ran through my mind. I considered mentioning her mismatched gams, but my throat tightened, and I choked on my words. I coughed in an attempt to clear my throat.

She smiled, knowingly as if she had, in fact, stopped the words from exiting my mouth. "I'd like to share with you an old gypsy legend," she said. "It's about a magician and his table."

"Have you heard the story of the magician's table before?" she asked.

"No," I replied. I tried to stand and walk away. Instead I remained riveted to the chair. My heart raced. I shook my head. The air grew thick, then thicker until it encased me in goo the consistency of heavy syrup. I felt sick like I was drowning. The old woman turned toward Ethan and Gary. I tried to stop her. I moved so slowly. I couldn't make my limbs work. She waved an arm as if shooing away insects.

"I think I'll take Ethan to the park," Gary said. The creepy old woman smiled and nodded her consent as the two of them walked away and left me alone with her. I tried to scream for them to wait, but again my words lodged in my throat. She continued to wave the boys off in the direction of the park as though she controlled their movements.

We silently watched as they disappeared from view. She firmly patted the table in front of me. When she did, the air cleared and I no longer felt encased in liquid.

She patted the table once more to regained my full attention. "I use my table for magic," she began. "Therefore my table has been fashioned on the principles of the magician's table," she continued as she caressed its surface.

She paused while I shook the remaining residue of the thickened air from my ears. "The first leg represents trust in God's goodness," she said. She glanced up at me, studied me for a moment, then seemed satisfied and went on.

"The second leg stands for health and strength of body."

She paused for a moment then continued, "The third leg signifies competence in the realm of coins. To desire prosperity is not evil. Money when balanced in harmony with the other three legs is, in fact, essential to the magician's table."

"Finally," she said, "we are faced with the fourth and final leg of the magician's table. This leg represents the shared knowledge of the ancestors and the teachers who have gone before us." She peered up and furrowed her brow. "It is not necessary to learn every lesson personally and the hard way. That is by choice. Hmm."

She stopped abruptly and studied me. She intertwined her fingers then rested her nose on her fore-fingers and her chin on her thumbs. "You have a choice to make." She pursed her lips and watched me as she patiently waited.

My mind exploded in chatter. *Somehow this strange old woman knows I'm sick —— and broke —— and a hard learner. What does she want from me? I didn't ask for her voodoo crap, yet she's describing me. My life! She thinks that three legs of my table are in bad shape, and she's right.*

*Holy Crap! Crap, Crap, Crap! What am I supposed to do now?*

*As I see it, I have a couple of choices. The easiest and first choice would be to do as I've always done, my favorite thing, nothing.* As I contemplated this option, the image of the old women's gnarled limbs popped into my mind. *Has she been bent and twisted by a life without balance? Will that happen to me? Has it already? Man, my feet hurt.*

*If I cut out everything else, what do I believe to be true? Is the grand Creator of everything good, bad or indifferent? Indifference is the absence of caring.* I searched my soul for the truth — for my truth. *What did I believe?*

*I could believe God is no good. I could simply blame God for my misfortune. If I give up the belief that God is good, I could cut that leg down to size. Although all the legs would be shorter, I could again have a table able to stand on four legs — minimized, but sturdy. That would bring balance. The trouble is, I don't like to settle. And, I can't blame God for my current predicament.*

In fact, I felt kind of badly. Considering the pitiful condition of my table that I'd neglected for so long, I was struck by the awareness of God's patience in the face of my neglect.

*So, then, what am I left with? I'm left with a lot of work. I need to rebuild three crumbling legs. I think I'll work backward. I need to gain some knowledge and understanding from those who have gone before me. I can do that. That actually sounds fun and exciting. Good. Then I need to see money as a beneficial balancer instead of the root of all evil. And I need to figure out how to earn some of that coin on my own. That's going to be a little more difficult, but not impossible.*

*Lastly, I have to live. I have to kick cancer in the pants and live. This small matter I'm already working on. Maybe I'll try to fix them all at the same time. I don't have to figure out the logistics right now. Right now I'm sitting at a wooden table on the front lawn of some strange old woman's house. We've never met before, and I think I've overstayed my welcome.*

*Yes. I will fix my table.*

As soon as my mind quieted the old woman spoke: "You have chosen well."

*How could she know I'd chosen well?* I asked myself. *I didn't even know that.*

She leaned forward and grabbed my hands. Her strength and agility stunned me. I tried to pull away, but she was too strong. She turned my hands over palms up. As she studied my palms, she spoke rapidly, earnestly: "Remember, once you have started down this path you must **not turn back!**"

"Do not lose faith! The greatest wretchedness known to man is the evil he is capable of once he has lost his faith," the old woman added.

I pulled my hands away. She was scaring me.

She slumped back in her chair. She sat for many moments with her eyes closed.

Then she sat up and began to shuffle a deck of cards. She placed them in front of me. Without knowing why, I took the deck and I began dropping cards into small piles. I then picked up all the piles and handed her back the deck. She placed ten cards face down in the pattern of a cross on the table. She turned over the first card and held it in her hand. She smiled as she studied it. "To become the Magician," she said, "you must be young and old. Enthusiastic and experienced. You must have gotten your teeth and still be willing to use them."

"I don't want to be a magician," I protested.

She smiled as though she knew me better than I knew myself. "Soon you will have to choose one of five paths." She ran her hand over the nine remaining cards on the table. She looked up and studied my face for a long time. Instead of turning over another card, she deliberately placed the cards one by one back in the deck and gently wrapped the deck in a beautifully hand-embroidered scarf. She set the small bundle off to her left. "The choice is yours and yours alone." She folded her hands and placed them in her lap. "Choose wisely."

"Now, go ——— speak to River," the old woman commanded as

she pointed a crooked finger off behind me to my left.

I'd been dismissed.

I wanted to see my boys. As I stumbled off toward the park, I realized I never paid the strange old woman for her services. I turned around to offer her some cash, or at the very least to thank her, but she was gone.

CHAPTER 41

# RIVER

B efore I went to find the boys, I had the urge to visit the Waving Girl. She stood high atop the bluff overlooking the Savannah River. Her name was Florence Martus. Although the actual girl was long gone, a bronze likeness of her still graced the river's edge. The inscription below her monument read: "Her immortality stems from her friendly greeting to passing ships, a welcome to strangers entering the port and a farewell to wave them safely onward."

For most of her life Florence lived with her brother, George, in a little cottage on Elba Island near the Savannah Inlet. While George kept the Cockspur Island Lighthouse, Florence waved her scarf by day and her lantern by night. It's estimated that she greeted more than 50,000 ships during her life on Elbe Island. It may seem insignificant, but for a simple kind gesture to all ships passing her way (not just the expensive ones or the large ones or the ones that flew flags she recognized) Florence Martus stands larger than life as a beacon of kindness to us all.

I closed my eyes and felt the cool breeze kiss my face as I stood next to Florence and her collie. I removed my scarf and together we waved to the river.

*Well, I guess, before I go find the boys, I could see if the river feels like chit-chatting,* I said to myself. I chuckled at the mere thought of it.

I descended the steps leading from the bluff to the river. As I neared the banks, to my surprise, the old river began to hum. I sat down on a park bench near the banks, and swayed gently to the music. The hum lulled me to sleep.

River found his voice and began to sing. He sang of his life and all he had seen.

He sang of an old gypsy woman and her conversation with a traveler. He sang of my table, my garden and my life. I discovered that I actually wanted to talk to River.

I opened myself up and his song seeped into my veins. Silent tears fell from my eyes and mixed with his muddy water. As my essence mixed with his, he thanked me for my gift.

My left eye traveled around the back of my head before settling next to my right eye. I could no longer breathe the air. I had been transformed into a fish. I needed to enter the water or suffocate.

"Ah, a flounder," River commented. "Come, swim with me."

I flopped and thrashed, finally reaching the shelter of the river. I tried to breathe through my mouth at first. I gasped and sputtered. Then my gills instinctively kicked in. I inhaled deeply and began to relax. Soon we lazily floated along together. "Why do you go so slowly?" I asked.

"Meander," he replied.

"Pardon me?"

"I **meander**." He corrected me once again.

"Oh, yes, of course, meander. Why do you meander?" I asked as I shook my head. *I'm a flounder playing semantics with a river,* I added under my breath in bewilderment.

"To where am I headed?" He answered my question with a question of his own.

"To the ocean," I replied.

"What happens then?"

"What do you mean?"

"I mean what I say. What happens then?" River countered my question once more.

"Well then, that's it, I guess," I replied.

He laughed a hearty, rolling laugh, sending me rippling off the bottom. "Then, what's the rush? Only upon meeting the sea does the young river realize that he is no-longer a river," he added.

"Me? I'm old. I'm not in such a hurry. I flow steadily toward the ocean, but I also weave from side to side. When I get there, I'll be happy to once again be the ocean. But, for now, I like being a river. So, I take my time."

"Why do you sometimes turn so far that you're back to places you've been before?" I asked.

"For perspective and reflection. I get an opportunity to see myself as I was, from where I am," River replied. "I've learned a lot from the meander. When I double back I can view my earlier life from outside the banks in which those events live. It's an important perspective to me. I see me, from me, but no longer immersed in me. I think it's good to look back and to see myself, as I was. It helps me remain tranquil, more content with who I am, and perhaps this self-reflection even helps me appreciate the rocks I was forced to go around. Once I merge with the ocean, I won't get the chance to see myself in this way — apart."

"I get it," I said. "So you can see yourself from the outside." I nodded almost imperceptibly as I tried to wrap my head around the words of a talking river.

"Exactly. Also, I found as I lean, in order to get a better view of a flower or a tree, the bank often gives way — inviting me to take a closer look. This bending slows my flow and allows me to linger. In exchange I bring some of what was the bank with me to the ocean. It's what I do. My job is to pick up bits and pieces of what I've experienced along the way. In the end I bestow my collection to the ocean as my gift for having lived. My experiences provide nutrition to the ocean and the life therein. Do you understand what I mean?"

My head was swimming.

"Let me explain it to you this way. What color is my water?" River asked.

"It's brown."

"What is the color of the young river?"

"Clear. Clear is clean and much prettier than brown." I felt smart. I knew the answer to this one.

"Perhaps, but, think for a moment. When you were younger you loved to mix all of your Play-Doh colors together. Do you remember?"

"I do, but how do you... ?" I paused and shook my head. "Never mind."

"After mixing all of the colors together what color did you ultimately end up with? Do you recall?"

"I do. It was brown. I called it pooh-pooh brown."

"It looked brown and yet you and I both know that your ball of brown dough contained fire engine red, hot pink, lime green, army green, sky blue, three shades of yellow and a white."

"It is the same with me and my water," River continued. "In my murky brown water I see the sky-blue of the glacier stream. I see the vibrant-green of the floating duckweed. I see the blood-red of injured animals who mended their wounds in my healing waters. I see the burnt-orange of autumn leaves once scattered on my surface."

"When I finally reach the ocean, "he added. "I will offer up myself knowing that my beautiful brown water awakens the ocean with the memories and colors carried therein. And I'll know that Ocean is pleased."

I thanked River for helping me see the beauty of his brown water and for helping me embrace my new slower pace of life.

"You're welcome," River replied

My fins once again grew fingers and feet. As my gills closed and my lungs expanded, I made my way for shore.

*EDIBLE:*
*Good to eat,*
*and wholesome to digest,*
*as a worm to a toad,*
*a toad to a snake,*
*a snake to a pig,*
*a pig to a man,*
*and a man to a worm.*

——— Ambrose Bierce

CHAPTER 42

VAMPIRES

I dragged myself, drenched and drained, back onto the bank. I collapsed beneath a weeping willow tree and once again became accustomed to the air. River continued to hum as he rolled leisurely onward.

I warmed my bones in the setting sun, recounting all the things I'd learned from River. Hermes sat down beside me. As I dried in the warm air of sunset, I reached up to scratch an itch. To my surprise, three long, dark masses emanated from the crown of my head. They hung down below my shoulders. Believing they must be my hair, I tried to comb out the snarls. The smooth eel-like creatures wiggled and writhed at my touch.

To my horror, parasitic lampreys had attached themselves to me. Undetected, they grew long, thick and well-fed.

"Get them off!" I screamed.

"You have to do that yourself," Hermes stated.

I jumped to my feet and ran around in circles. Hermes quieted me. He pointed to a dense grove of trees in the distance. There in the dim light, a group of people began to gather and huddle closely in the shadows of the thickly wooded stand.

I forgot for a moment about my parasitic lampreys and focused my attention instead on the people gathering in the trees. "They seem so tight-knit," I said and patted Hermes on the arm.

Together we watched. "They must be extended family," I added.

"Sh-h-h-h. Watch and listen," he said as he put a finger to his lips.

Many of the people gathered there looked weak and sickly. *What are they waiting for?* I asked myself below my breath since Hermes told me to be quiet.

Soon a tall, blonde woman in her mid-forties arrived. In contrast to the others she appeared as though she had just come from a spa — vibrant, radiant and healthy. Pleased with her arrival, they stood-up and formed a line. Each in turn greeted her with a tight hug then plunged sharp fangs deep into her neck.

I jumped up and hid behind the trunk of the willow tree. "Holy shit! Did you see that?"

"Sh-h-h," Hermes said as he smiled and once again placed a finger up to his lips.

Together we watched in silence as the beautiful woman gracefully arched her head out of the way and allowed the other members of her clan to feed on her. They continued in this manner until she looked as hollow and pale they did. The ones at the end of line were forced to go hungry.

"What in the hell is going on here?" I asked Hermes. I wanted to run away, but the scene fascinated me.

"What does it look like?" he retorted.

"Why did that woman allow the vampires to feed off of her?"

"She's part of the clan. They are the unlucky ones — unable to find a host of their own. In order to feed her family she returns, freshly engorged from her host, and shares what she has consumed with the others."

"They're killing her!" I exclaimed.

"No. They'll only feed as long as she has more than they do, then they'll stop."

"Then what?" I asked as I brushed the wriggling eels over my shoulder.

"Why don't you just remove those things?" Hermes asked.

"What? I asked you a question. What happens then?"

Hermes sighed and continued, "Then someone will have to go out from the clan and find a new host."

"How is it done?"

"Don't you know?" Our eyes locked for an uncomfortably long moment before we both turned and continued to watch the scene play out.

As I watched, I felt struck by the indifference in the woman's eyes. Her lifeblood had just been sucked from her in a relatively short amount of time. Yet, she didn't seem to care.

"Hey, Hermes, she looks familiar to me," I replied

"You feel drawn to her," he said.

"No," I said as I held my hand up to stop his words. "I am deeply mortified by her behavior!" I flung the eels over my shoulder. "I am mortified by the behavior of every last one of them!" I pushed Hermes words back with both hands and grunted.

The others, satiated for the night, dispersed. Tired, depleted and alone, she sat down beneath an Elm tree to rest. She looked directly at me. Her face held no expression.

"I recognize her," I uttered in astonishment.

"I thought you might," Hermes said smiling with satisfaction.

"But she doesn't know me," I puzzled. Then ever so slowly, I began to recognize myself. "I am her host," I gasped.

*The clever cat eats cheese and breathes
down rat holes with baited breath.*
——————— W. C. Fields

CHAPTER 43

# HOSTS

Why didn't she recognize me?" I asked Hermes. "We've known each other for so many years."

"Vampires have been trained for more than a lifetime of lifetimes to spot a host," he explained. "It's what they do. Picture it this way: You are at a train station. You're waiting for a train. Any train. It doesn't matter where the train is going or how long the ride is. You wait until you spot a train with a flag in the window. Let's say the flag bears the emblem of an eel on it. That's the train you've been waiting for."

Hermes paused and stared at the top of my head for an uncomfortably long time before continuing, "now, if a train shows up at the station without an eel in the window, would you recognize that train?"

I didn't answer.

"Would you recognize it even if you had traveled many miles on that train before?" Hermes asked.

"Well, that doesn't make any sense," I said as I scratched my head. An eel wiggled at my touch. "AARRRGG, I can't stand these pesky creatures!" I screamed, as I pointed to the top of my head with eight fingers.

"Then take them off," Hermes replied. He looked mildly amused as he crossed his arms and watched me struggle.

And, struggle I did. I struggled with the eels, with Hermes train and with his words; most of all however, I struggled with the thought that I had willingly been the vampire's host.

"I don't have time for your nonsense," I countered, attacking Hermes verbally. "Why would I wait at the station for a train to take me to: I don't care where, for I don't care how long?"

"Simple. The ride is free."

"Hmmm," I pondered for a moment. "Where is this train going again?"

Hermes shot me a look. His eyes betrayed his thoughts. "Weren't you listening at all? I answered that question for you once already." He inhaled deeply, exhaling slowly before he replied, "It ——— doesn't ——— matter."

"But it does matter," I countered. "It matters to me." My voice cracked as I grappled with a side of myself I didn't want to face.

"No, it doesn't."

Hermes could see I was trying to understand. He placed his hands on my shoulders. He turned me slightly. We faced each other. He looked into my eyes.

"Vampires have chosen to be passengers," he continued. "They made that choice long ago. Life, for them, is not about the destination. It's about the free ride. They are very good at finding a free ride, but they must be invited."

"Are you kidding me? No one in her right mind would willingly play host to a vampire!" I raged.

Hermes chuckled. "Really?" He raised his eyebrows as he assessed my indignation with moderate amusement.

"Vampires need the lifeblood of others. They cannot exist without it," he continued calmly. "Therefore, they are always on the lookout for a host," he paused and looked at me deeply.

I reached up to scratch a nagging itch on top of my head. "Ugh, these obnoxious eels are driving me crazy! Hermes, do you have a rubber band or something I can tie these things back with?"

"Why don't you just remove them?" He spoke slowly, deliberately.

"You're no help."

Hermes shook his head. "We both know that vampires are very charming creatures," he said. "Unlike in the movies however, the host has to encourage the vampire to feed on her. In other words, the host has to willingly invite the vampire to board her train."

"I get it already!" I exploded. "You're telling me that this," I threw my arms up-and-down and around in circles, "is my fault! That I asked her to feed on me! That I begged to be bitten! Well I say, bull, Hermes! I say bull crap! 'Cuz that's what you are full of! You are full of crap!" I roared as I stomped off. I had no idea where I was going. I just kept stomping until Hermes disappeared from view. When I was sure he couldn't see me anymore, I stopped stomping.

I bent over to catch my breath. My mind reeled as it went back to the clan of vampires. *What will happen to them?* I wondered. Even now I found myself feeling somehow responsible for their welfare. *If I refuse to be a host, who would feed them?* But, —— I didn't want to be a host anymore.

Frustrated, I snatched up the eels dangling from my head and laced them together in a thick braid.

My illness had brought me to a place where I felt I needed every drop of blood I had.

While I struggled with my role as host, Hermes rejoined me. He placed a hand compassionately on my shoulder. "They'll survive. There's safety in numbers. And after all, vampires are charming; remember? I'm sure one of them will snag a host in no time," he said. "And it's okay. It's just one of the many dances of nature — perhaps primitive, but not wrong. It just is. "

"Well, I don't like it," I said.

"Then don't do it."

"I won't!"

If you choose not to be a host, why not start with those?" he pointed the eels hanging from my head.

"Don't think I won't!"

"Then do it."

"I will! See this?" I grabbed the thick braid of eels and ripped them from my head. It hurt a little, but then I felt much better — more energetic — more alive.

"Alright! Nicely done!" Hermes clapped his hands together in victory.

*Why had I waited so long?*

CHAPTER 44

# PERSPECTIVE

A clap of thunder startled me. I awoke on a park bench near the banks of the Savannah River. The sun had already dipped below the horizon. *I had better go find my boys and get back to the motel before the rain hits,* I told myself as I rushed off in the direction of the park.

That night as I readied myself for bed, Hermes words echoed in my ears. You **invited** her in. You **begged** her to come. You **wanted** to be the perfect host.

She was my friend. We'd known each other since third grade. She phoned. She had lost her husband; she'd lost her job; she'd lost her house. My heart went out to her. She had nowhere to turn. I **invited her in.**

I volunteered to fly out and drive the two thousand miles back to my home — just she, I and her big dog. I **begged** her to come.

I made her life so comfortable, that, in her own words, she couldn't imagine being anywhere else. **I was the perfect host.** *Darn it. Hermes was right.*

I began to think she'd never leave. Days turned into weeks that turned into months.

One particularly warm August day, my down-and-out friend returned home bearing food in a white paper bag. She wanted to talk. I pulled a ham and cheese submarine sandwich from the bag and cut it in half. I grabbed a bottle of Mexican Coke and a can of Diet Pepsi from the fridge. We retired to the front porch. As we ate we watched the people in cars, drivers in semi trucks, squirrels and blue jays all busily collecting their nuts.

She wanted to talk about dreaming mainly — more specifically about having dreams. When we'd finished eating, she pulled a light gray pack of cigarettes out of her pocket. She lit one and leaned back. She placed her feet up on the ginger-colored ottoman that rested between our wrought iron rockers. She closed her eyes and exhaled. A circle of smoke the same color as the cigarette package danced through her long, blonde hair.

"Let's open our own coffee shop," she began.

"Where?" I asked excitedly.

"It doesn't matter." With perfectly manicured fingernails, she brushed the question aside.

"Well, actually, it does. Location is super important."

"Can't you ever just shut-up and listen?" she said as she opened her eyes and glared at me.

"Well, if we're going to do this thing, we need to know where, don't we?"

"I'm dreaming." She closed her eyes and although she still sounded annoyed, she seemed to calm down considerably.

Relieved and cheery, I replied, "Me too!"

"**No! You're not!** Dreaming means I just want to talk about doing stuff I know I'll never do," she said. "I don't want your ——— help ——— or concerns ——— or questions!"

She stood and began pacing back and forth on the porch.

"You do this every time! You take my dreams and try and fill them with —— **reality!**"

She let out an audible *harumph* of frustration.

Obviously I'd missed the mark when I thought she'd calmed down. Puzzled, I retraced the conversation as though I were watching an instant replay of a pivotal moment during a tennis match. I scratched my head.

"Don't you get it?" she said and threw her hands up in frustration at my ignorance.

"I think I'm beginning to," I replied. In an effort to hold my tongue, I gripped the iron arms of my chair and squeezed. I leaned forward and I looked down at my hands. I watched the color leave my knuckles. I'd never been particularly good at holding my tongue. It took quite a bit of effort.

I'd recently discovered, however, on the rare instances when I listened more and talked less, I occasionally learned something. Oh, it all happened rather by chance. Or it could have been by design, I'm not sure. Disease and treatment had left me tired. And because of this I'd experienced brief lapses in time when I couldn't find the strength to talk. *Who knew other people had such interesting and insightful things to say?* I wanted to hear what she had to say about dreams. So, I resisted the growing urge to talk and remained silent. Perhaps I could learn something.

I did.

I learned that many people never intend to pursue their dreams. Those people like their dreams unachievable. I learned that in such cases one should never mistake a dream for a goal. It ruins the dream.

Although I'd learned all of this and much more, I couldn't resist the urge to ask, "Are you sure we shouldn't at least try to open a coffee shop?"

"No!" she replied emphatically as she opened the screen door to the front lawn and flicked her spent cigarette at an unsuspecting chipmunk. She then turned and stood in front of me with her hands on her hips.

She was tall, but from this vantage point, she looked positively Amazonian and birdlike. She bent forward at the waist and tucked her head between her shoulders.

"Listen here," she began. "Since you obviously don't get it, I'm going to spell it out for you. When I'm dreaming, just shut-up and listen. If you have to talk say, 'That sounds great!'"

"I'm never going to do any of these things. I'm not even sure I want to. For a little while I just want to think about what it would be like. That's all. That's why it's called **dreaming**."

Her voice ended in a high-pitched squawk, which only reinforced the disturbing image from my mind's eye of her as a carrion bird waiting to pick my bones clean. Her hands still on her hips, she slowly moved her elbows forward and back.

"I'm sorry," I replied rather meekly. Inside I added, *please, don't eat me.*

"Anyway, I gotta go." In a flurry, she picked up her purse, and she left. As she pulled out of the driveway and turned right, she passed by the house once more. I still sat on the front porch. She didn't wave. She didn't even look in my direction.

As I watched her drive away, I began to think that perchance she was taking advantage of me. She always had enough money for cigarettes, the lottery and fast food, but never for groceries, rent or utilities. I shrugged it off. She wouldn't take advantage of me. We were friends since the third grade and friends wouldn't take advantage of friends.

As naïve as it sounds, until recently I thought words and their meanings were somehow universal. I thought a friend is a friend is a friend. Love is love and dreams are dreams. But they're not. These words mean tremendously different things to different people.

Like favorite recipes for comfort food, the resulting product remains loosely recognizable, yet the exact ingredients, intensity and texture vary vastly from person to person.

Dreams? Ah, my favorite recipe in the card box. Dreams are

reservations. Some people make a reservation, but never get to the restaurant. Some never intend too. Others go to the restaurant, read the menu, but just don't eat. There exist those among us who actually plan for the occasion.

These remarkable minority creatures, chart a day of fulfillment. They mark that date on the calendar and even preplan a route to the restaurant and how they will dress for the occasion. This last group of dreamers probably already knows what they'll order. After all, they've been dreaming of this moment for a long time.

I discovered love is as individual as chili. Some like it hot and spicy. Others prefer it subtle and subdued. Made with beef or chicken — corn or noodles, with or without beans. It's all chili — it's all love.

Friendship, on the other hand, resembles more of a meatloaf. And as much as you try to follow a recipe no two meatloaves ever turn out the same. Regardless of the shape or size; sauce or no sauce; meat or meatless; meatloaf must represent comfort food even when it occasionally gives you heartburn. If it's not ultimately comforting and reassuring, consoling and uplifting, it's not meatloaf, and it's not friendship.

Now, I was sick. The doctors, in treating my illness, made me feel worse. I needed some consoling, some uplifting, but it didn't come. For over thirty-five years I thought we were friends, but the recipe no longer worked for me. I removed it from my card box. Not wanting to discard it, I carried it with me. I secretly hoped that through teamwork, together we would make the recipe for our friendship work. I couldn't fix it alone.

Finally, after many months, I threw the recipe in the trashcan and I asked my friend to leave. It would take many more months for her to actually detach herself from me and go. It would take years for me to stop mourning the loss of a friendship that never existed.

Inside my mind Hermes clapped his hands together in victory once more. "Alright! Nicely done!" I heard him say.

*Happiness depends upon ourselves.*

———— Aristotle

## CHAPTER 45

# TURTLE AND THE RACE CAR

The next morning we packed up the rental car and headed south from Savannah along the Atlantic coastline — destination Amelia Island, Florida.

Gary had been stationed near there during his Navy days. While on route, he filled our minds with tales of giant, prehistoric shark teeth washing up on the beaches.

Ethan bounced around in the backseat. "Are we there, yet? I'm going to find the biggest shark tooth in the history of the world!" he exclaimed as he excitedly pulled on the back of my car seat.

We arrived early afternoon, checked into a quaint motel and walked down to the beach for some sun, sand, surf and sharks' teeth.

As I soaked in the natural beauty of the Appalachian quartz coastline of Amelia Island, I gazed out over the vast Atlantic Ocean. Turtles and race cars traversed my mind.

I remembered my mom telling me about her laps around the track at the Daytona 500 speedway in a stock car. I couldn't recall the name of the driver or the number of his car. I decided to give her a quick call and find out. I dug around in the dark, scratchy, winter-wool, shoulder bag that basked in the sun next to me. I picked up my phone. The screen read EMERGENCY CALLS ONLY. *How weird?* I thought. *That's never happened before.*

As I contemplated my options, I watched my husband try to teach our son how to bodysurf. I considered how badly I wanted to know the name of a NASCAR driver or the number of his car and finally decided it probably wasn't an emergency.

Ethan and Gary glided along toward shore until the small waves gently broke and curled against the white, sand beach. Behind them two brown pelicans floated lazily on the sparkling swells. Beyond the breakers a third pelican dove in for a tasty morsel of fish. Dolphins lunged and plunged only to reemerge further down the beach. April on Amelia Island was a balmy 85 degrees. I put my phone back into my Pendleton bag, the one with the orange and black Southwestern design.

My skin, still cracked and crisp from radiation, I pulled my hood down low and stretched the sleeves of my shirt to cover my hands. Sheltered from the sun's radiation, I wished to soak in the ocean air. I longed to throw off all my protective gear and bask in the sunshine, but I contented myself by admiring the dolphins as they dove and danced still further toward the horizon. I breathed in deeply the briny sea air and for a moment got that illusive all's-right-with-the-world feeling. I closed my eyes and developed a mental snapshot of the scene. I never wanted to forget this moment. "Beautiful," I said to myself and placed the imaginary snapshot into my pocket.

(But now I forgot where I was going with this story.) Oh right, I was musing over racetracks, race cars and turtles.

Racetracks are banked at the corners. The banks are steep. So steep, in fact, that you have to go no less than (Now what was it? 120? Or was it 140 miles an hour? Oh, I forget... Let's suffice it to say really, really fast or you'll lose traction and slide backward off the track. What I mean to say is that it's logistically impossible to remain on the racetrack and slow down. So, we're left with two options:  Go fast or get off.

I pictured myself in my fast machine. Life on the track, was, wow, exhilarating! Go! Go!  I just passed Harvey. What's my standing? I was in third place. I sped up. Driver number 24 blew a head gasket. He's out of the race. Poor sap. That just means less competition for me. I'll have my agent send a card, but I don't have the time to really care. I'm in third place. If I slow down I may drop back to fourth or worse yet, seventh.

I pulled into the pits for a quick overhaul then it was back on the track. Driver 62, trying to gain his standing too fast, over-invested in the turn. He's never going to negotiate it. He clicked driver number 31. They both spun out of control. Four more cars were taken out in the aftermath. The race was down to me and, well, me. I was in first place.

To hold that lead, I had to stay alert. I needed to concentrate solely on staying ahead. The pressure was immense. Only thirty laps to go, 29, 28... I have got to hang on. Finally I saw the checkered flag. I burned through the final lap. Elated, I roared across the finish line ——— or was it the start line? Wait a minute? Where am I? I've won, but I've gone exactly ——— nowhere. I've seen nothing.

Personal growth? Are you kidding me? Do you have any idea of the heat? The pressure? The G force? The stress? I've just traveled 190 miles an hour. Forever. I've lived the same stretch of road 200, maybe 300 times. Wait just a doggone minute. I've just ended up exactly where I started.

In contrast, I'd like to introduce you to my little friend, Arvelis Parsley. Arvelis is a lazy, little turtle. Most turtles live a very long time, but Arvelis is sickly. She's only got perhaps eighty turtle years to live. You see, the poor sap got cancer and the doctor says she's not going to make it. Arvelis likes to walk. She walks slowly — not in a straight line, but in a general direction.

If she's hungry, she leisurely grazes then naps in the sun awhile. When she feels rested and ready, she continues on her journey. As far as she can recall, none of her fellow turtles has ever blown a head gasket, although Jim got himself hung up in some fishing line once. Arvelis stopped and helped poor Jim with the mess he found himself tangled up in. She gave him the turtle high five and headed leisurely on her way.

Arvelis Parsley travels slowly — around a third of a mile an hour. Some hours she logs no miles at all. In a day she travels conservatively two miles, but she doesn't travel every day. In an entire week she'll have traveled perhaps only ten miles.

Our friend, sickly, little, slow-motion Arvelis doesn't race against the clock. And still, in a single year she will have seen 520 miles of varying landscapes. She will have experienced new sights, sounds, smells and tastes. She'll have met creatures she'd only seen in picture books.

By mid-life, at this pace Arvelis will have traveled more than 20,000 miles. She's spent time with her family. She's cared deeply for her friends. Where she could, she stopped and helped. She's not sure where she's heading, but she listens to her instincts and continues in an approximate heading. She grows a little wiser and her life is enriched by the variety of her days. In eighty years, Arvelis Parsley comes near the end of her unimportant, unmotivated life — a life filled with 41,600 unique miles of varying sites and experiences.

The moral of this story? It's never too late to leave the rat race. If you leave the track, with only five years left, at turtle speed, you can still experience 2,600 undiscovered miles. In one day you can enjoy two wonderfully new miles. If you find you have one hour left to live, one hour still grants you a third of a mile. A third of a mile may not seem like much, but a third of a mile from the racetrack the air smells sweeter, less like motor oil, less like burning rubber, less like exhaustion. The roar of an over-wound engine is but a distant memory. What I'm trying to say is, if you have an hour left on the planet, it's not too late to experience life off the track. Breathe deeply, my friend.

CHAPTER 46

# PACKAGED DEALS

The really memorable moments in life come prepackaged. Each package contains something valuable and some — well — for lack of a better word — crap. Beautiful arrives with horrifying. Magnificent rolled in mundane. Balanced. I think it's for stability during shipping or it could be for *stickability*. Each package must be dissected, examined and evaluated. Only then can we better decide which parts are worth keeping, nurturing, growing; which parts should be discarded; and which parts require further excavation. Some packages we unwrap right away. Others wait until a time when we are better equipped to glean their value from within. Unfortunately many packages are discarded as worthless before we've had a chance to unlock and collect that nugget of goodness.

One Christmas my mom received a beautiful present from her sister. We all admired the care with which the gift was decorated and tied. I played Santa that year. After all the other presents had been opened, I handed mom the loveliest package from under the tree. She smiled warmly at her sister and thanked her for such a beautiful present. She took the pretty package and carefully untied the bow.

As she removed the paper, her expression changed from anticipation through bafflement to finally rest at obvious disenchantment.

For inside this gorgeous façade were white paper plates. Not fancy designer ones — no Chinet. The gift contained the kind of cheap, flimsy, white paper plates with the fluted edges you need two of just to carry a slice of Wonder bread to the toaster.

I can't recall what my mom received for Christmas from her sister any other year. The exquisite beauty of the packaging on this particular holiday burned the thoughtlessness of the gift into my memory.

I returned from my memory and watched from a rocky outcropping as Ethan skipped through the surf and cheerfully sang to himself out loud. When he wasn't singing he was talking. I soaked in the scene and closed my eyes. The image healed me or at the very least put me at ease.

He hunted for sharks' teeth in the hardest-to-reach spots on the beach. I couldn't help but chuckle to myself. I recalled an unopened package given to me by the Snowman over thirty years ago.

I closed my eyes and watched as the Snowman sauntered down the hallway to the long, narrow window of my third-grade classroom. I hurriedly collected my belongings. We were going fishing! He was a tall man from the hip to the shoulder — his torso long and strong. His legs, however, appeared to be four inches too short for the rest of him. They bowed from the hip outward to the knee then back in to meet at the ankles. He walked slowly, and as he strolled, he swayed gently from side to side. Together we walked to his two-toned green Ford F150 Super Cab pickup truck.

We drove off in the direction of Rome, Wisconsin. We stopped at Larry's Boat Livery for some dew worms. Then we drove to Richy Oldenschlager's house. The Bark River ran through his backyard — just below the dam. I brought along my new, bright-orange fishing rod — the one with the push-button Zebco reel.

In no time at all, my bait dangled from the lowest branch of a cottonwood tree. I had been trying to cast into the shallows near the opposite bank of the river. I just knew all the fish were lined up on the far shore and I was going to catch me one of them.

"Watch the other fishermen," the Snowman urged. Usually he was a man of few words. *Why had he picked now of all times to become so chatty? Couldn't he see I was trying to snag the big one?* I just threw him an exasperated glance. I secretly hoped he'd stop talking and let me fish. No such luck.

"Note," he continued to my dismay, "how the fisherman from the shore works, struggles, casts, reels and recasts. He's trying to throw his bait out into the deepest water possible."

I rolled my eyes and tugged and whipped my pole frantically from side to side. *Why is he talking instead of untangling me from the tree?* I wondered.

"Now look at those guys," he said pointing to two men fishing from an aluminum rowboat. "D'ya see how they pull into the shallows and cast toward the banks? Since they're in a boat, they think all the fish are close to shore."

Finally he stopped talking and untangled my line for the seventh time. I cast. Reeled. Cast, reeled and cast again.

"You know what the key to catching fish is?" he asked, trying a different approach.

"No." I eagerly awaited his reply because I really wanted to catch a fish.

"Keep your bait in the water." His voice carried an edge.

*Was he mad about something?* I wondered. I turned up my nose and furrowed my brow. "Very funny," I replied. So far, I'd only used up thirteen worms. "Darn it!" I stomped my foot. "Dad, I'm stuck in the tree again!"

He took my pole and tried to free the thirty-foot cottonwood from the line. The tree already wore a matched set of hooks, line and sinkers. A pair of bobbers dangled from her branches like earrings. You could call them a gift, from me to the tree.

Without another word, the Snowman took my new, bright-orange rod with the push-button Zebco reel and tossed the whole enchilada into the river. Although he was a man of few words, he was a man of even less patience.

I guessed we were all done fishing. Luckily, my line was still caught in the cottonwood tree. It stopped my pole from floating too far down stream. I ran along the bank and snatched my pole out of the river. I sprinted back toward the truck. Fortunately we were pan-fishing. When I hit the end of the six-pound test line, it snapped leaving another set of hook, line and sinker up in the tree.

I hurriedly packed up my tackle box, threw everything in the bed of the pickup and jumped into the passenger seat. We drove home in silence. The next time the Snowman took me out of school to go fishing, he brought along two cane poles.

As I recall, my Zebco reel was never the same. The Snowman and I fished many times. Sometimes we sat on the banks and dreamt of fishing. Sometimes we actually got our bait wet. Most times are but a warm and foggy sketch on my memory. Our day on the banks of the Bark River in Richy Oldenschlager's backyard, however, remains etched in detail in my mind. Frustration burned so hot a Snowman had a meltdown.

As I watched our son struggle for sharks' teeth in nearly impossible to reach locations, perceptive good sense hidden beneath the sting of a Snowman's fury was no longer lost on an eight-year-old. At forty-three, I finally comprehended and appreciated the insight he tried so hard to bestow. It's all the same river. If you want to fish close to shore, fish from the shore. If you want to fish in the deep water, put your boat in the deep water. It only takes a cane pole and some common sense.

I had carried that unopened package with me for over thirty years. The gift remained buried in hurt and resentment until I was ready to reach through the pain and excavate the kernel of wisdom below. Because the Snowman threw my pole in the water the experience wasn't lost. I can now actually appreciate his fire. One seemingly mean-spirited gesture gave the memory more sticking power. For that I am grateful.

Anticipation followed by insignificance or wisdom wrapped in anger; that's the *Upside of Down*. Both events changed me in ways that wouldn't have worked without the juxtaposition of opposites. That's the balancing act for shipping and receiving.

I closed my eyes and could again see my bright-orange fishing rod. I noted the push-button Zebco reel. I saw a cottonwood tree adorned with bobbers, sinkers and dew worms. I imagined telling Ethan that he's making it harder than it has to be. But not today. He's only eight. Maybe when he's eighteen or twenty-eight, but not today. Today I'm an observer.

Ethan ran up to me. "Mom, I found the inner ear bone of a whale, a hairy scallop, four petrified leeches and some barnacles," he exclaimed, but no sharks' teeth, yet.

Behind him a snowbird with twin, triple D's hanging from her chest wall strode through the sand. My mind turned to Betty.

*She wore a short skirt and a tight sweater
and her figure described a set of parabolas
that could cause cardiac arrest in a yak.*

Getting Even ——————————— Woody Allen

CHAPTER 47

## BETTY'S BOOBS

Yes, Betty was blessed with a bodacious set of knockers. That was, until the day her beautiful breasts, to quote a werewolf, "betrayed her". Her surgeon recommended removing them both and replacing them with either silicone or saline bags. The choice was hers. These implants would have to go underneath the chest muscles and, ladies and gentlemen, I'm pretty sure it is impossible to cram two watermelons underneath the pectoral muscles.

Betty trusted her doctor's opinion and moved forward with the surgery. A cosmetic surgeon placed expandable inserts underneath her chest muscles. Within a week the expander on the left failed. Although she returned weekly for saline injections, the left side refused to grow. Her body quietly absorbed the leaching saline solution.

Months filled with chemo and radiation passed. After her last radiation treatment she met with her plastic surgeon again. "I want my boobs now," she requested.

"You need at least six months to heal after radiation before I can even consider placing your permanent implants," he explained.

She waited. Finally the day arrived when she would receive her new and improved ta-tas. Nipples she dangled in front of her husband like a carrot for a horse. If he quit smoking, she'd get nipples. I'm not sure where Betty's nipples will come from. Perhaps from the inside of her thigh or they could be prosthetic. Her husband shows no signs of giving up the smokes. So, I'm pretty sure Betty has plenty of time to nipple shop. The areola, that darkened area around the nipple, will eventually be tattooed on and, voila, breasts.

After the second surgery, a silicone implant rounded out her right breast like a wide, high, seat cushion she could rest her chin on. A matching implant unfortunately refused to cram beneath her under-expanded left pectoral muscle. The plastic surgeon had to install a second expander on that side. Betty would have to wait many more months until she received her matched set.

Mere weeks after this surgery, her right breast became red and inflamed. She ran a fever. After a short visit to her surgeon she was placed in the care of an infectious diseases doctor. He scheduled ten consecutive days of intravenous antibiotics.

The antibiotics worked wonders. After only six infusions the doctor placed her on an oral dose. However, her permanent implant now had a fifty-fifty chance of failure.

According to the infectious diseases doctor, any foreign object inside the body increases the chance for infection. Bacteria can cling to that object and create a barrier around itself which renders antibiotics ineffective. Infections can travel from an ingrown toenail, for example, to a breast implant. Unless Betty lives in a plastic bubble, the fifty-fifty chance of failure is always present. Some doctors estimate the failure rate even higher – especially if you've had radiation.

If you or someone you know faces breast surgery, get as much information as possible. Surgeons know a lot, but not everything. If you plan on sticking around for a while, it may be to your benefit to research the long-term success rates of all the options presented.

As of today, Betty still awaits her matched set of boobies.

*I do not know whether I was then a man
dreaming I was a butterfly, or whether
I am now a butterfly dreaming I am a man.*

—————— Chuang Tzu

CHAPTER 48

# WHO ARE YOU? II

I could feel his words lightly touch the backs of my ears. As they circled round and round me, I didn't turn. I couldn't run. I just stood with my back to him frozen in space and time. *After all these years, please, not again,* I said to myself and pinched my eyes shut.

Behind me, that darned caterpillar repeated, "Who are you?" He danced and he waited.

Instinctively I knew, this time, I either had to find the answer he sought or be silenced forever. But I still didn't know who I was — not really. *Think. Think,* I scolded myself. But, I couldn't think. I didn't have the answer he was looking for and I couldn't come up with anything clever to say. *How did I get myself into this mess?* I wondered.

"Looking for answers — that's how." A calm, quieting voice answered from my navel. Over the past few months I'd grown quite accustomed to my naval speaking to me. *True enough,* I replied and patted my tummy. So at the very least I knew why I was here. I started from there — which is to say, I started from here. And, here is always the best place to start.

I turned slowly to face the caterpillar. He looked adorable! He wore a pale, straw cowboy hat, three sizes too small for his fat little head. A navy blue cord drawn up tightly under his chins kept the cowboy hat in place. A tarnished-tin sheriff's star twinkled from his fringed-rawhide bolero vest. A lariat slung neatly from a holster he wore low on the hip – if caterpillars have hips that is. He swung his rope round and round like a cowboy. More amazingly still, he was good at it. He could gracefully run his entire chubby body through the rope without getting entangled in it. I smiled in spite of my fear.

"I too want answers Mr. Caterpillar," I began tentatively. "So I guess you could call me a ——— a seeker ——— an old-fashioned seeker."

He grinned a toothy, leaf-cutting grin. "Go on. Oh, and, by the way, you can call me Bob." He holstered his lasso and crossed his front six legs across his chest. He assessed me with great amusement and a slight amount of interest.

"I am... I am..." I shook my head and my eyes flipped backward — inward. Inside, the sun shown brightly as white, puffy clouds floated by. The landscape rolled out low, lush, green and dewy.

The small child inside me now stood on her lotus flower. She had her back to me, facing instead a large, brick wall.

As I walked toward her, I called out. She turned and our eyes met for just a moment.

"Finally," she sighed. "You've come at last. She smiled, relieved, and plucked her thumb from the wall. "You have to take over now."

I tried to scream as the wall I'd built and a tsunami of words and emotions came rushing over me.

My eyes flipped back to the outside world. My lips parted and I spewed, "I am an ancient child. I am weak and rigid — malleable and brittle. I want to feel safe, yet independent. I long for freedom and security. I am stubborn, slow and insistent. I am impetuous and impatient! Are you happy now? What more do you want from me?"

"That's all very fine and good, but, who are you?" The caterpillar, unruffled, wistfully moved a hand up to his chins as he awaited my reply.

I sat down and closed my eyes. I inhaled deeply as his words swirled around me once more.

*Exhale,* I reminded myself. Like the river I began to see myself from the outside. "To my mom and the Snowman, I am a daughter," I slowly began. "To Gary, I am a wife. To Ethan, I am a mother. To the doctors, I am a patient. To the reader, I am an author. To the audience, I am a musician. To my friends, I am a friend. I am all of these things — and yet, I am more."

I grasped the caterpillar's chubby cheeks in my hands, "and to you, dear sweet Mr. Caterpillar ——— I am you. And you are me.

"You're doing great. You're on the right track. Finish it!"

"Who are you?" he asked me one last time.

"To me?" I asked.

"To you," he replied.

"To me, I am."

## I AM!

When I said those two magic words the last pieces of my jigsaw puzzle fell into place and I sensed the energy that animates us all. I am whole. I am life. I am eternal. I am one with the spark that initiated and taught the egg to hatch.

## I AM!

I could finally see that all I wanted to be already exists inside of me. It always has. All I needed to do was believe in myself and allow me to be who I am.

The caterpillar gave me a solid nod of approval. No longer would he be bound to the earth. He transformed and flew away.

"Bye, Bob." For the first time in my life, I would miss my antagonist. I closed my eyes and lay back. I floated in the blissful sea of Happy.

"You'll never be completely rid of me," Bob called back, "I'm part of you."

"I'm glad," I replied.

*Ahhh, happy — what a wonderful emotion,* I thought.

I heard again the Snowman's words: "All that really matters is that you are truly happy." With my eyes still closed I smiled and whispered, "I am." I don't know if the Snowman could hear me, but I like to think he did.

CHAPTER 49

# EDNA LEAVES

April 28, 2010. I awoke early. I heard a rustling in the downstairs bathroom. I got out of bed to investigate. I grabbed my miniature Milwaukee Brewer's baseball bat from the backstairs — the one I received on fan appreciation night. I left all the lights off. I raised the bat over my head in the ready-to-strike position and tiptoed down the stairs and around the corner. In the dim glow of the night-light I could see Edna June. She stood on a narrow ladder which she had propped up against the sink. She was rummaging through my medicine cabinet.

"Edna, what, in the world, are you doing?" I asked.

"Me?" She glanced over the top of her dark-rimmed glasses. "I'm stocking up," she mentioned distractedly. "Plenty of people are going to need me you know."

She stopped for a moment and shrugged before continuing, "I thought you wouldn't mind. Most of this stuff you won't use anymore," she added as she tossed numerous objects from my medicine cabinet into her doctor's bag. "It beats throwing them in the trash."

"Are you leaving?"

"My work here is done." Edna closed her bag but left the door to my medicine cabinet open. She climbed down her ladder and waddled toward me. It still scared me when she did that. She skittered up the leg of the kitchen table. When she reached the top, she motioned for me to join her. I took a seat.

"You were a good opponent," Edna began. "You discovered much and battled hard. Never forget what you learned." She leaned in close. "Secretly, I hope to never come back here," she added. "But I will be watching you."

"Good-bye, Edna," I replied with relief and gratitude. "I hope we never meet again. Where will you go?"

"Don't worry about me," she said as she patted her hips as if she'd misplaced something. After looking around she shrugged, snatched up her doctor's bag and repelled down a thin translucent thread to the floor.

Once on the ground she folded her hands together as if to pray, and bowed deeply. "Farewell," she said.

"Thank you," I replied as I mirrored her movements.

When I looked up again, she was gone.

In the morning, on the kitchen table, I found a tattered and torn picture of a little girl in a calico sundress and rubber boots. A snowman looked on as she snatched up water bugs, frogs, minnows and crayfish in the shallows. I turned the picture over. "Never forget," was all that was written.

*Pursue some path, however narrow and crooked,*
*in which you can walk with love and reverence.*

———— Henry David Thoreau

CHAPTER 50

# BURNING BRIDGES

Hermes had walked many miles with me over the past months. He stopped. "From here," Hermes said, "you have to choose your path. Alone."

"Are you leaving, too?" I asked.

"I've taken you as far as I possibly can," he replied. "The next steps you must take alone," he remarked, his voice serious and full of concern.

"Piece-o'-cake," I responded. "I know my way from here and anyway I have a couple of friends who are going to meet me just around the bend." Excited and happy, I hugged Hermes and jogged off to meet my friends.

"Good-bye and good luck," Hermes said. He sounded uneasy.

I waved to him over my shoulder.

*He's going to miss me,* I sang to myself as I happily trotted off.

In the distance, just around the next corner, five pathways converged. I knew this point well. I had been there many times before. Planning to see my friends, I arrived where the paths met, but nobody was there. Bewildered, I walked in a circle and looked down each of the paths.

I stood in the center and recalled how I stood in this very spot one year earlier. I recalled how tired I was. I recalled how the cancer and subsequent treatment had taken every ounce of energy. I recalled how alone I had felt.

Then I recalled how a familiar voice called out to me from the first path. "Hello, friend. Come, see me."

"I am so tired," I replied. "Could you meet me here instead? We could have a cup of coffee together or something."

"Oh, I'm sorry, I can't. I'm broke," the voice from the first path replied. "But if you could come here, I'd love to see you."

For a moment I had considered taking that first path. I had walked it many times before. I knew it well, but I didn't have the strength.

"I'm sorry I can't," I said. "How about instead we meet here in one year. Hopefully, in that time, you'll be able to save enough money for a cup of coffee."

"Sounds good," the voice from the first path replied and she was gone.

I looked at the second path. I recalled how a familiar voice from that path called out to me: "Hello, friend. Come, see me."

"I'm exhausted," I remembered replying. "Could you meet me here instead? We could have a cup of coffee together or something."

"Oh, I'd love to, but I have to work," the voice from the second path responded.

"I'll be back through here in a year. Perhaps in that time, you'll be able to schedule a day off. It would be great to see you," I remembered saying.

I remembered the loneliness I felt as I gazed at the third path, and how a familiar voice called out to me: "Hello, friend. Come, see me."

I wanted my friend by my side, but, for the first time, I couldn't find the energy to make the rest of the journey to her place. "Could you please meet me here instead?" I remembered the desperation in my voice.

"Oh, it's much too far, she replied. "Couldn't you just come here?"

I couldn't understand how the path was longer in one direction than the other. For the first time, the distance was too far for me. "I'll be back this way in a year," I responded. "Perhaps you will be able to make the trip by then."

Now I stood at this crossroads alone. I had taken the brunt of a horrible journey without them.

I hadn't been alone, and I knew that. I had my husband and my son. I had my mom and many new friends. I had acquaintances and strangers, who supported me in many wonderful ways I could have never before fathomed. And to each and every one of them, I am truly grateful. Knowing all of this, I still wanted my friends by my side.

I was sure they were each just somehow delayed. I believed at least one of them would soon arrive. *Perhaps they are just running late,* I reassured myself. I sat down and waited. I waited an hour. No one came. Then a day. Still no one. I began to feel cold and lit a fire. Days turned into weeks. Still no one came. A month passed and my loneliness and sadness turned to anger. I waited another month. As I waited alone, my anger turned to fury.

I grabbed a burning log from my fire. I methodically set the ropes and tresses of the bridge that led to the first path ablaze.

Raging with hurt and anger, I lit the second bridge and then the third. I sat back and watched them burn. The bridges to the familiar paths on which I'd spent so much of my life fell in ruin. I collapsed in the ashes, wounded and exhausted.

Two paths remained: the one I had just endured and the one I had never ventured. This new path appeared foreign and foreboding. I could only see a few feet down the trail. Paralyzed by fear and by what I had done, I sat down and closed my eyes. A vivid vision came to me.

I could see my friend from the world of the first path. She was happy. She hadn't noticed the burning bridge at all. She was busy living her life.

Then I saw my friend from the world of the second path. She played with her dogs, her phone by her side. She too hadn't noticed that the bridge that once connected our worlds was gone.

Lastly I could see the world of the third path. She too was busy enjoying her life.

Truthfully, the damage wouldn't affect their lives at all. I no longer felt sad or angry. Forgiveness wasn't necessary. I silently wished them happiness.

I turned around for one last look at this crossroads I would forever leave behind. Hermes stood at the edge of the path we had walked together. He waved to me. "Pleasant journey" He called out across the distance.

I waved in return and headed off, apprehensively, into a world of grand adventures, big trees and rain.

CHAPTER 51

# BIG TREES AND RAIN

Big magnificent trees lined my new pathway.

My head ached. My stomach twisted in knots. I wasn't sure I could keep down my breakfast croissant. I looked up at the awesome giants that flanked me on either side as a fresh, cleansing rain began to fall. Soon the smell of burning bridges was replaced with a faint perfume of trilliums. Although it was spring, fallen leaves still littered the forest floor. I closed my eyes as droplets of rain quenched my parched skin.

I had set-off alone. Soon my husband and son joined me. They had decided to travel this new stretch of road with me. For that I was overjoyed. The three of us hiked together in the cold rains of spring. Soon the trees thinned and a landscape of possibilities opened up before us. Together we explored wellsprings, marshes, swamps, ancient lake beds and ancestral encampments.

I heard a voice calling from behind me and fast footfalls on crunchy leaves. I turned around to see my friend from the second path sprinting in my direction.

"Wait for me!" she called out.

I had done enough waiting; I didn't want to wait anymore. I kept walking.

"I would have come sooner," she called after me, "but I didn't know what to do. You were so sick. I didn't know if you wanted company. I'm sorry. Wherever you are going, I want to come with you. Please, let me be part of your life. Please, let me come."

I stopped. I waited. She was not only my friend, she was family. I had missed her company deeply. I grabbed her hand and together we walked my new pathway. I knew it wouldn't always be like this. I knew she had her own roads to travel, but, for that time, I was overjoyed that she chose to join me.

In those cold, rainy days filled with nature and family, I began to heal and to dream of brighter days.

*Adventures don't begin until you get into the forest.
That first step is an act of faith.*

——————— Mickey Hart
Drummer from the Grateful Dead

*And I will show that there is no imperfection
in the present, and can be none in the future,
And I will show that whatever happens to
anybody it may be turn'd to beautiful results,
And I will show that nothing can happen
more beautiful than death,
And I will thread a thread through my poems
that time and events are compact,
And that all the things of the universe are
perfect miracles, each as profound as any.*

Leaves of Grass ————————— Walt Whitman

CHAPTER 52

# THE FINAL CURTAIN

Before reading this chapter, I'd like you to answer one question for me. How do you leave a party? Give it some time. Mull the question over. Be honest with yourself. Some people sneak out early when no one's looking. Others fall asleep in a chair and have to be awakened and informed that the party's over. There are as many different styles as people in the world and no one way is any better than any other.

I happen to be one of those people who says good-bye for an hour. I like to stand in the doorway. I like the view from the threshold. I enjoy the time to leisurely say "Good-bye" and "Thank you". I like to reminisce together about the evening's festivities. To have one more laugh together. One more hug, one last "It was great to see you."

That's why for me, cancer is the perfect exit strategy. I don't know if we get to choose the final curtain, but I do think we can learn a lot about what we may choose by watching ourselves leave a party or better yet a family reunion.

Who we think we are often has nothing to do with who we find reflected in the face of reality. What we think we want is often worlds away from what is really important to us. We often can't hear the voices of our hearts or of our souls anymore.

When death seemed hypothetical, I'd jokingly say, "Give me a nice aneurism any day." Having faced my own mortality, I know, if allowed, I'll choose to linger at the threshold. I'd like to give the out-of-towners a chance to arrive. I'd like to laugh just one more time. I'd like to dance with my husband one more time. I'd like to smell my son's hair one more time. I'll want to survey the scene and know that they'll all be just fine after I go. Then and only then can I squeeze the final exhale from my lungs and fly free. Then and only then can I leave in peace. Then and only then can I smile and slip silently through the veil.

## CHAPTER 53

# HEAVEN READY

H eaven has always created for me an image of chubby, naked babies with wings, lazily reclined on cottony, white clouds and gently strumming harps for eternity — not really my idea of a good time. In fact, the very thought makes me fear death.

During my journey, as I contemplated my demise, I worked on a way to become more enamored with the harp-playing cherub image of my Lutheran youth. First off, I didn't want to spend eternity as a naked baby. I preferred to become a fully alert, sentient being when I died. I'd still like to learn how to play the harp, but not just any harp — a magical harp with notes that mean something.

What if life after death is more quantum physics-ish? More string theory-ish? What if matter, all matter, plus space and time is really nothing more than energy vibrating at different pitches? What if I get to play that harp? Now there's a harp I could spend eternity playing. When I get my turn at the harp I will create a short-lived but impressive fad — vehicles with 87 cup holders.

I'm still not sure I'm ready for that final journey called death, but at least I'm packed. Death can be a spur-of-the-moment traveler. He might not give me the time for that one last "I love you" before we blastoff. If I have the opportunity to tell someone — I take it. Whenever Death decides to call, I'll be ready. "Just a minute," I'll say. "Let me grab a sweater and my ready bag." He may pop by tomorrow. He may wait 45 years. I feel honored that Hermes helped me pack in advance.

"Hermes!" I called out. "Let me see Heaven. I don't want to stay. I just want a quick look around."

Although he didn't speak, Hermes granted me my sneak peek, my preview of the afterlife. When I arrived, there were no pearly gates. Instead, a Jewish grandmother sat at a well-appointed, well-organized reception desk.

"So, how was life?" she asked as she shuffled through her paperwork. (She couldn't seem to find my documents.)

She didn't wait for a reply. "Tell me all about it. Did you have a good go-round, Sweetie?"

"Where's the tunnel? The pearly gates? The light?" I asked avoiding her question. Only Hermes and I knew that my go-round wasn't finished yet. It was our little secret.

"I get that question all the time," she said as she waved a hand unceremoniously over her right shoulder. "Can you see the campfire?"

I glanced in the general direction of her gesture. Behind her, firelight danced and flickered. I nodded.

"That's your first stop. They're all telling stories. I hope you have some good ones."

I patted my bag. "I've got a few." I replied.

As the dying embers of firelight joined with the rising sun my image of heaven faded. "Thank you!" I whispered to Edna, to Bob, to Hermes and to the Snowman as I greeted the dawn of a new day with great wonder and anticipation.

*Life is either a daring adventure or nothing.*
*Security does not exist in nature,*
*nor do the children of men as a whole experience it.*
*Avoiding danger is no safer in the long run than exposure.*

——————— Helen Keller

**THE UPSIDE OF DOWN**
C/O Parsley Publishing
PO Box 386
Palmyra, WI 53156-0386

www.parsleypublishing.com

# ORDER FORM

Name: _____

Address: _____

_____

_____

Phone: _____

E-mail: _____

|  | Quantity | Price | Total |
|---|---|---|---|
| **THE UPSIDE OF DOWN**<br>BY: KRISTINE DEXHEIMER |  | X  $13.95 | $ |
|  |  | Subtotal | $ |
| *U.S. add $4.95 S&H - $2.50 each add'l copy.*<br>*Outside U.S. add $8.95 S&H - $4.50 each add'l copy.* |  | Shipping | $ |
|  | Sales Tax (WI only, 5.5% = 0.77 /book ) |  | $ |
|  | Total Enclosed |  | $ |

Return to: **THE UPSIDE OF DOWN**

C/O Parsley Publishing
PO Box 386
Palmyra, WI 53156-0386

**Kristine Dexheimer** currently resides in southeastern Wisconsin with her husband of nearly twenty years and their ten-year-old son. She serves on the board of trustees of her local library and plays alto saxophone in the community band. When she's not writing, Kristine spends her days exploring, thinking, discovering, tending what she's planted and celebrating life.